Openings
for
Marxist-Christian
Dialogue

Openings
for
Marxist-Christian
Dialogue

THOMAS W. OGLETREE
editor

Nashville   ABINGDON PRESS   New York

OPENINGS FOR MARXIST-CHRISTIAN DIALOGUE

Copyright © 1968, 1969 by Abingdon Press

Library of Congress Catalog Card Number: 69-12768

SET UP, PRINTED, AND BOUND BY THE
PARTHENON PRESS, AT NASHVILLE,
TENNESSEE, UNITED STATES OF AMERICA

*For my students
at the Chicago Theological Seminary
who labor to unite intellectual rigor
with practical action for social change*

Preface

One of the most exciting recent developments in Christian theology has been the emergence of a dialogue between Marxist philosophers and Christian theologians. This dialogue is already beginning to have significant implications for the future shape of both Marxist thought and Christian theology. In recognition of this fact the Chicago Theological Seminary elected to devote its 1968 Alden-Tuthill Lectures to the implications this dialogue has for Christian faith and for the relation of Christians to Marxists and Communists. The present volume contains the lectures presented at that time. The lectures of Jürgen Moltmann, Charles C. West, and Paul Lehmann deal directly with theological issues arising out of the current dialogue. The lecture of Sidney Lens provides an overview of the "changing character of communism" that clarifies the social and historical context of the current possibilities for dialogue. The introduction seeks to set the dialogue in context by highlighting the developments within both Marxism and Christianity that have led to a situation of dialogue.

Contents

Introduction

THOMAS W. OGLETREE

That Christian theologians and Marxist philosophers should have anything to do with each other is unthinkable for countless numbers of people, both Communists and Christians. For many Christians, especially in America, communism means quite simply: Stalinist tyranny, totalitarianism, the cynical disregard for human dignity and for basic human values, an international conspiracy to subvert or destroy liberal democratic institutions, a fanatical commitment to gain dominion over the whole world either by deceit or by force. In short, communism is viewed as one of the principal threats to the well-being of men. By the same token, Christianity for many Communists means: the Inquisition, witch hunts, the suppression of free scientific inquiry, the cynical use of religious beliefs and practices both to justify the existence of oppressive social systems and to lull the oppressed into an acceptance of that oppression. In short, Christianity is identified as one of the principal barriers to human progress.

As long as Christians and Communists perceive each other in terms of these stereotypes—and both portraits have a real basis in fact—it is scarcely tolerable even to consider coexistence, let alone genuine dialogue. Dialogue requires an openness to the other, a readiness to learn from the other, to be changed by the other. It stems from a desire on the part of the dialogue partners to grow through mutual interaction, to develop a deeper self-understanding in community with each other. Movements which see each other as unmitigated evils cannot in good faith entertain the prospect of dialogue. They must oppose each other to the bitter end. Yet significant new opportunities are opening up at the present time for a joint exploration of the basic convictions and vital concerns of both Christianity and Marxism, a fact that reflects not a surrender of integrity, but a willingness on the part of some Marxist philosophers and Christian theologians to look behind the sinister mask of the other to the creative sources of value and commitment.

It is scarcely necessary to note that a positive and constructive encounter between Christianity and Marxism is not new. From the beginning Karl Marx and Friedrich Engels drew much of the inspiration for the humanitarian thrust of their work from Christianity.[1]

[1] Cf. the essays, articles, and excerpts under the heading "Humanitarianism and Liberalism of a Young Hegelian," *Writings of the Young Marx on Philosophy and Society*, trans. and ed. by Loyd D. Easton and Kurt H. Guddat (Garden City, N.Y.: Doubleday, 1967). Hereafter cited *Young Marx*.

Engels seems to have maintained his fascination with Christianity throughout his life, for he continued to study and analyze theological writings, particularly those dealing with primitive Christianity, long after the basic elements in an essentially negative assessment of religion were well established.[2] Though Marx himself increasingly focused his attention on the formulation of a rigorous social theory centering in problems of political economy, the basic values that informed his thought continued to reflect the impact of biblical faith on Western civilization. Even in the realm of practical politics the Communist Party has on occasion found it expedient and appropriate to call upon Christians to join with it in a common struggle for a more humane social order.[3]

By the same token, Christians have been repeatedly drawn to the writings of Marx, Engels, Lenin, and other Marxist thinkers, because their own commitments sensitized them to the social problems these men were seeking to understand and overcome. Actually, the Christian interest in various forms of socialism antedates Marx.

[2] Cf. such studies as *The Peasant War in Germany, Dialectics of Nature, Bruno Bauer and Early Christianity, The Book of Revelation,* and *On the History of Early Christianity.* Excerpts from these and other writings of Marx and Engels on religion are conveniently collected in a single volume, *Marx and Engels On Religion* (New York: Schocken Books, 1964). Hereafter cited *On Religion.*

[3] The most important instances are the appeal of Maurice Thorez in 1936 to the Catholic workers to cooperate with Communists in the workers' struggle in France as a part of the "popular front policy," and the invitation of the Italian Communist Party for Christians to join in the fight against fascism in 1936 and 1938. In 1945, the Italian Communist Party opened its membership to all persons without regard to religion or race.

13

Quite apart from experiments in communal living by religious orders, there have been Christians since the beginnings of the industrial revolution who have seen in socialism the only practical solution to the human misery precipitated by a new social order.[4] The originality of Marx lies not in the fact that he projected a socialist vision of society, but in the fact that he sought to ground that vision in a theoretical understanding of the laws of social development. In America, one of the most important instances of Christian interest in Marxism is found in the Fellowship of Socialist Christians, which, under the leadership of Reinhold Niebuhr, drew heavily upon Marxist insights in seeking an appropriate Christian response to the social and economic crisis that gripped American society during the thirties.[5]

In spite of these precedents, we have just passed through a period in which little or no fruitful interaction between Marxists and Christians was possible. That new openings for the Marxist-Christian encounter are developing at the present time is largely a consequence of changing conditions both within communism and within the church. Sidney Lens points to some of the changes taking place within the communist world

[4] One of the most important instances of this interest is Claude Henri de Saint-Simon (1760-1825). His study, *Le Nouveau Christianisme,* proposed an economic order close to socialism on the basis of Christian principles.

[5] See the "Statement of Principles of the Fellowship of Socialist Christians," in *Christianity and Society,* XI (Winter 1945-46), 33-37. For an excellent study of Niebuhr's relation to Marxism, see Charles C. West, *Communism and the Theologians* (New York: Macmillan, 1958), pp. 117-76.

which have created a situation for dialogue.[6] Chairman Khrushchev's speech denouncing Stalinist excesses at the Twentieth Congress of the Communist Party can appropriately serve as a symbolic event to represent these changes. The essential point is that the present situation both within the socialist block of nations and within the various national Communist Parties allows for the possibility that Marxist thought can be liberated from the shackles of dogmatism and restored to a significant critical function. A critical form of Marxist thought can interact constructively with alternative perspectives on man in a common quest for creative ways to deal with new developments in human society. In this setting a number of distinguished Marxist philosophers, most notably Roger Garaudy, Ernst Bloch, and Milan Machovec, have opened up fresh lines of inquiry that constitute invitations to Christian theologians to engage in dialogue.

If we seek to identify major happenings within the church that manifest a new openness to dialogue, we can point most appropriately to the proceedings of the Second Vatican Council and to the Geneva Conference on Church and Society sponsored by the World Council of Churches (Summer, 1966). The former embodied a drive within Roman Catholicism to bring the Church up to date, primarily by calling it to grapple in a fresh way with the problems and concerns of the contemporary world. The latter represented a growing conviction within Protestantism that the meaning of Christian existence must be expressed in relation to the technical and social

---

[6] "The Changing Character of Communism," in the present volume.

revolutions of our times.[7] This common orientation to the contemporary world is the most promising feature of the current stage of the ecumenical movement, for in centering attention on the Christian promise to the worldly concerns of men, it renders obsolete many of the issues which have previously divided Christians. At the same time, the renewed determination to address the modern world in its concreteness can only have a hollow sound if it does not include genuine openness to contemporary forms of the Marxist challenge. In view of these circumstances a growing number of Christian theologians, both Protestant and Roman Catholic, are giving fresh attention to Marxist writings as a part of their effort to become responsible participants in the current debate about the future of man.

Serious dialogue between Marxists and Christians is presently concentrated in a number of European centers and in certain countries of Latin America. The European discussion is the more theoretical, involving a critical exploration of basic philosophical and theological questions. The theological essays in the present volume represent an attempt to explore and advance that discussion. Important practical considerations do underlie these conversations. In addition to the manifest desire to achieve a more satisfactory rapprochement between Eastern and Western Europe and with it a more stable mode of coexistence between communist and noncommunist states, there is a concern to understand and address more adequately the human problems that are common to modern industrial societies, whatever their

<hr>

[7] The theme of the Geneva Conference was "Christians in the Technical and Social Revolutions of Our Time."

pattern of social and political organization. However, pressing practical issues are much closer to the surface in Latin America. Many Christians in Latin America see no meaningful hope of progress for their countries apart from violent revolution. This conviction thrusts them into interaction with Marxists and Communists as they seek to clarify their own role and the role of the church in the historical struggles of men.[8]

The impact of the dialogue is just beginning to be felt in the United States. Here it is providing a stimulus for a fresh analysis and assessment of Marxist writings in light of the situation that currently prevails both within our society and within the life of the world at large. It gains its urgency from the necessity of understanding and responding creatively to the emergent black revolution in America's cities, and from the importance of examining critically the present stance of the United States in world affairs, politically, economically, and militarily. It can nourish the quest for a life style that faithfully expresses the Christian promise to the world in the

[8] The most striking instance of a Christian commitment to revolutionary action is the decision of Fr. Camilo Torres, the extraordinary social leader in Colombia, to leave the priesthood and join a guerrilla band. He was killed in 1966. His death is still an inspiration to the guerrillas, one group of which calls itself "the Fifteenth of February" to commemorate his death. More recently, Fr. Blase Bonpane and Fr. Thomas Melville, Maryknoll priests, were suspended and asked to leave Guatemala for their alleged revolutionary activities. Fr. Bonpane described his position toward Marxism as follows: "I don't believe you've got an immense amount of difficulty in establishing a bridge between Marxism and Christianity. I think that bridge is already being built and I think that Christianity has a lot to give Marxist thought and Marxist thought has something to contribute to our understanding of Christianity." *The National Catholic Reporter,* Jan. 31, 1968, p. 7.

context of the upheavals and uncertainties of our age.

Roger Garaudy has described the changing relations of Marxism and Christianity as a movement "from anathema to dialogue." [9] My task is to sketch briefly the main outlines of the developments within both Marxism and Christianity that embody this movement and that contribute to the possibilities of dialogue.

Marxist Openings to Christianity

The understanding of Christianity that became characteristic of the mature thought of both Marx and Engels took its starting point in the work of Ludwig Feuerbach. For Feuerbach, Christianity is an expression of man's alienation from himself, the objectification of the human essence in a supernatural realm. Man takes those qualities of human nature which he regards as intrinsically good and projects them outward in such a way that they are taken to be the qualities of a Divine Subject who exists independently of man. For Feuerbach, the qualities attributed to God by man do merit the label "divine." Nonetheless, they are actually man's own qualities, now celebrated and adored as the perfections of the Divine Being. The unfortunate consequence of this religious projection, according to Feuerbach, is that man in his exaltation of God alienates himself from himself, from the qualities which make up his own life. He impoverishes himself in order to enrich the being of God. Feuerbach's recommendation is that man over-

[9] *From Anathema to Dialogue: A Marxist Challenge to the Christian Churches,* trans. by Luke O'Neill (New York: Herder and Herder, 1966).

come his self-alienation by reclaiming his own qualities, by recognizing and embracing explicitly the human essence of religion. The result is not the end of religion, but a self-conscious realization of a religion of humanity.[10]

Marx endorsed Feuerbach's contention that man makes religion, including God and the entire realm of the supernatural.[11] He also appropriated and developed Feuerbach's analysis of the alienation involved in religious projection. However, he did not seek to replace theistic religion with a religion of humanity. In his judgment, religion is inescapably a form of "mystification." It obscures man's perception of the realities of his situation and hinders his effective action in the world to bring about humanizing social change. Consequently, man's liberation from religious alienation finally depends upon his liberation from religion as such. More important, Marx sharply criticized Feuerbach for ending up with a highly abstract notion of humanity, one that interpreted the being of man in isolation from the concrete social and historical conditions which shape his life. Such an interpretation is itself a form of self-alienation. In contrast, Marx emphasized the fact that man is a producer, a maker, and an agent of historical change. To gain an adequate understanding of man, including his religious life, it is necessary to attend to the factors that determine the concrete conditions under which man

---

[10] Cf. Ludwig Feuerbach, *The Essence of Christianity*, trans. by George Eliot (New York: Harper Torchbooks, 1957), pp. 29-30, 46 ff.

[11] From "Toward the Critique of Hegel's Philosophy of Right," *Marx and Engels: Basic Writings on Politics and Philosophy*, ed. by Lewis S. Feuer (Garden City, N. Y.: Doubleday, 1959), pp. 262-63. Hereafter cited *Basic Writings*.

acts, that set the possibilities and limits for such action.[12]

By emphasizing the concrete conditions that shape man's being, Marx, more than Feuerbach, was able to account for the emergence of religion in human experience. Religion, he noted, expresses both a real distress and a protest against that distress. It represents man's attempt to cope with the forces of nature and history that threaten to overwhelm him. As such, the questions and concerns it embodies are in no sense illusory. The difficulty is that the religious man creates a fantasy world for interpreting and dealing with the actualities of the real world. In this connection Marx speaks of religion as an "inverted world-consciousness." [13] It compensates in an illusory way for the suffering and anguish of life in this world. As a result, genuine understanding, the kind that can lead to real solutions to real human problems, is hindered or even rendered impossible.

Engels picked up Marx's contention that religion stems from genuine human distress. He sought to show that vital religious movements are fundamentally the struggles of oppressed and exploited peoples to realize a new life. In spite of their religious forms, they mask a tangible, earthly interest. He once suggested that the closest thing in the modern world to primitive Christianity is the working-class movement. He spelled out some of the similarities: (1) Christianity was a movement of oppressed peoples, a "slave religion"; (2) it preached sal-

[12] Cf. Marx's "Theses on Feuerbach," esp. theses IV through VIII. Available in many collections of Marx's writings. See *Basic Writings*, pp. 243-45. On the same point, see Engels' study, "Ludwig Feuerbach and the End of Classical German Philosophy," *On Religion*, p. 316. Cf. also pp. 237-47.

[13] *On Religion*, p. 41.

vation from bondage and misery; (3) though it believed itself to be engaged in a bitter struggle with the most powerful forces in the world, it was confident of total victory; and (4) though its adherents were persecuted and baited as enemies not only of the state but of the whole human race, it continued to forge ahead. Unfortunately, however, its revolutionary import was dissipated by the fact that it located man's hope of salvation not in a historic and this-worldly future, but in a heavenly world to come. In this respect it differed sharply from the emerging class consciousness of the modern worker.[14]

The picture is somewhat different in the case of the Reformation. There religious convictions were linked with revolutionary social and political change. Still, Engels argued that the driving forces behind these movements were tangible, earthly interests even though they presented themselves under the guise of religion. Luther's efforts at reformation were rooted in the rising interests of the burgher class in German society. Calvinism gave religious sanction to the emergence of the bourgeoisie, in turn reinforcing the struggle for a liberal democratic state as the form of state most congenial to the interests of the bourgeoisie.[15] Of greatest significance to Engels was Thomas Münzer, a leader of the left wing of the Reformation in Germany.[16] The religious elements in

[14] "On the History of Early Christianity," in *On Religion*, p. 316. Cf. also pp. 330-38.
[15] Cf. "Introduction to Socialism: Utopian and Scientific," *On Religion*, pp. 300-303.
[16] Cf. "The Peasant War in Germany," *On Religion*, pp. 103-17. Ernst Bloch has called Münzer the first theologian of revolution. Cf. *Thomas Münzer als theologe der Revolution* (Frankfurt am Main: Suhrkamp Verlag, 1921).

Münzer's efforts at reform provided only a thin disguise for the material interests of the peasantry, for he summoned them to seek "heaven" in this world by mobilizing for revolutionary action. The result was the well-known peasant's revolt. Engels contended that Luther's strong support of the brutal suppression of that revolt was motivated not by theological considerations, but by his personal identification with the economic and political interests of the rising burgher class in German society.

While religion has on occasion been associated with genuine revolutionary movements, Marx and Engels still considered it to be primarily a barrier to human progress. On the one hand, it causes the downtrodden to acquiesce in the face of oppression and exploitation, to seek the fulfillment of life not in a real struggle for historical change, but in an illusory world created by the religious imagination. "Religion is the opium of the people." [17] Engles noted how frequently the European bourgeoisie, following the uprisings of 1848, insisted that "religion must be kept alive for the masses." [18] Experience had taught them that religion has a strong stabilizing influence on workers and peasants. The British industrialists went so far as to cover the expenses for a Moody-Sankey revival in order to turn the attention of British workers away from their grievances to more spiritual matters. On the other hand, religion provides a sacral legitimation for the established order, no matter how just or unjust it may be. Paul's own words quite aptly illustrate Marx's point: "Let every person be subject to the governing authorities. For there is no authority ex-

[17] *On Religion,* p. 42.
[18] *Ibid.,* p. 313.

cept from God, and those that exist have been instituted by God. Therefore, he who resists the authorities resists what God has appointed" (Rom. 13:1-2 RSV). Because religion is characteristically allied with the present order, an attack on social evils necessarily involves an attack on religious authority as well. Marx once observed that the criticism of religion is the beginning of all criticism.[19] His point is that once we are free to challenge sacral authority, we are free to challenge any kind of social arrangement which oppresses or alienates men. Under these circumstances, the final liberation of man from economic exploitation and political oppression requires his liberation from religion itself.

Marx and Engels rejoiced in the developments within Western civilization that were bringing about man's emancipation from religion: the emergence of modern science, the historical-critical study of both the Bible and the traditions of the church, and, most especially, the increasing self-consciousness of revolutionary social movements. On this last point Engels attached special significance to the French Revolution, for it was the first revolutionary movement which "entirely cast off the religious cloak" and fought its battles on undisguised political lines.[20] The developing proletarian revolution likewise held the promise of being guided by a clear-headed, purely secular assessment of the real factors operative in advanced capitalist nations and of the revolutionary role of the workers in that situation.

Given their understanding of the essentially regressive role of religion, Marx and Engels would have found little

[19] *Ibid.*, p. 41.
[20] *Ibid.*, p. 305.

sense in a dialogue with Christian theologians. Even if such a dialogue produced no harmful results, it would at least be a diversion from the business at hand. At best, religion is a useless encumbrance destined to pass away with man's "coming of age." At worst, it is a barrier to human progress which must be vigorously opposed. In any case, Marx increasingly concerned himself not with philosophical and theological questions, but with problems of political economy. Likewise, the subsequent impact of his work centered in economic and political theory and in political programs seeking to utilize that theory both in revolutionary action and in the reconstruction of the basic institutions of human society. Generally speaking, there is little evidence that either Marx or his disciple were aware of the latent theological content which is invariably present in the theoretical and practical treatment of social processes. This oversight is not surprising, since Christianity is not in the first instance a social theory, even though it cannot legitimately be separated from social questions. The significance of the current readiness of Marxist philosophers to dialogue with Christian theologians is that it constitutes an acknowledgment of the presence of theological considerations in Marxist thought and a recognition that Marxism has in part functioned in a manner that is equivalent to a religious perspective.

Doubtless many factors have contributed to the current openness to Christianity exhibited by some Marxist philosophers. For one thing, modern developments in scientific and social thinking have not brought about the demise of religion as Marx and Engels anticipated. Especially noteworthy has been the ability of Christian theologians to reformulate the themes of faith in a way that is compatible with modern scientific thinking. Unquestionably Christianity has been significantly altered by the emergence of science, by biblical criticism, and by the epochal changes that have taken place in human society during the past one hundred years. At the same time, it has in some of its expressions manifested considerable capacity to respond creatively to these new developments. Indeed, for many persons the new forms of Christian life and thought represent a revitalization of faith. The realistic Marxist thinker finds it necessary to reflect critically on the fact that religion may have an enduring role in human experience, a fact that necessitates a revision of the traditional Marxist analysis of religion. The "Testament" of Palmiero Togliatti, the late General Secretary of the Italian Communist Party, reflects such a reappraisal:

The old atheistic propaganda is of no use. The very problem of religious conscience, its content, its roots among the masses, and the way of over-coming it must be presented in a different manner from that adopted in the past if we wish to reach the Catholic masses and be understood by them. Otherwise our outstretched hand to the Catholics would be regarded as pure expediency and almost as hypocrisy.[21]

More important, from the standpoint of the central Marxist concern, is the recognition that religion is not necessarily an opiate, that in some circumstances it may even be a leaven. Roger Garaudy has put the point strongly: "The thesis that religion always and everywhere turns men away from struggle and from work is in

[21] Quoted by Harvey Cox in "The Christian Marxist Dialogue: What Next?" *Dialog,* VII (Winter, 1968) , 22.

flagrant contradiction to the facts of history." [22] In one sense, Garaudy's statement departs in no way from the view of Marx and Engels. As we have noted, Engels knew that religion could be associated with active efforts at social change. Besides, Garaudy himself is firm in his insistence that religion is still allied for the most part with the oppressors rather than the oppressed. Even so, his suggestion that religion may be a leaven of change does move beyond the traditional Marxist critique of religion. It does not simply say that religion sometimes functions as a *disguise* for tangible, earthly interests in a revolutionary struggle; it suggests that religion may be a *contributing factor,* an enabler, in that struggle.

Ernst Bloch and Roger Garaudy have both taken fresh looks at the roots of Christian faith in order to identify the source of its potential as a leaven of change. Their judgment is that the eschatological expectation of Christianity introduced a new factor in man's consciousness of himself and his possibilities in the world which converges with the Marxist understanding of man as an agent of revolutionary change. Indeed, Bloch acknowledges that the Marxist understanding itself derives from the eschatological thrust of biblical faith.[23]

In classical culture man was viewed as a part of a cosmic order that is essentially fixed and unchanging. In this frame of reference an expectation of the genuinely new, which can provide a basis for historical initiative,

[22] *From Anathema to Dialogue,* p. 100.

[23] Cf. Ernst Bloch, *Religion im Erbe: Eine Auswahl aus seinen religion-philosphischen Schriften,* ed. with an introduction by Jürgen Moltmann (Munich and Hamburg: Siebenstern Taschenbuch Verlag, 1967), pp. 66-69, 100-101.

can scarcely arise. The changes that do occur in human history are experienced as purely contingent, as directionless and without purpose. In some contexts change is even experienced as the deterioration of the cosmic order, leading inexorably to its total disintegration. Under those circumstances man's only hope is that a decaying universe can be reconstituted and restored to its primal form.[24] Biblical eschatology, in contrast, points toward the emergence of a qualitatively new future that breaks through the limits of the present evil age. It holds out the promise that the present age can be negated for the sake of a "new heaven and a new earth." This expectation leads man to understand himself as a man of hope, as a man open to the promise of a qualitatively new future. In that understanding, he is empowered both to struggle with his present world, even to contradict it, and to participate as a subject of historical initiative in the creation of a new world. The point of this analysis is that it suggests to both Bloch and Garaudy that biblical eschatology contains the root of a revolutionary stance toward reality, a stance that is basic to the Marxist vision of man.

Admittedly, Christianity's radical historical orientation was soon neutralized. Intellectually, this development occurred when Christian theologians appropriated Greek thought as the basic framework for interpreting the Christian message. Practically speaking, it occurred as the church, beginning with the Emperor Constantine (fourth century), allied itself with the ruling classes of

---

[24] For a discussion of this motif in archaic religion, see Mircea Eliade, *Cosmos and History* (New York: Harper Torchbooks, 1959), pp. 62-92.

society.[25] However, as Greek modes of thought give way to pragmatic and developmental ways of thinking, and as the church loses its favored position in society through the process of secularization, Christianity has the possibility of recovering and giving contemporary expression to the radical orientation that characterized its origins. It is this possibility that makes Christianity interesting to Marxist thinkers.

Under the present circumstances, Marxist participants in the dialogue with Christian theologians are not preoccupied with abolishing Christianity or even with merely learning to coexist with the Christian church, which may in any case manage to survive. They are interested in discovering what Christianity can contribute to the continuing development of Marxist thought. Garaudy identifies two themes in regard to which Christianity can supplement and enrich Marxism: transcendence and subjectivity. The first of these is closely related to the notion that man is an agent of change in the historical process. Garaudy speaks of Marxism as a "methodology of historical initiative." By that he means that the theoretical and scientific activity of Marx and his successors is oriented toward the concern to find realistic and practical ways to change the world. Marx expressed this concern succinctly: "The philosophers have only *interpreted* the world in various ways; the point, however, is to *change* it!" [26] Interestingly enough,

---

[25] Because of this alliance, Bloch's interest in Christianity has focused not on the mainline ecclesiastical tradition, but on the underground history of nonconformists from Marcion to the twentieth-century religious socialists. Cf. *Religion im Erbe,* p. 12.

[26] "Theses on Feuerbach," *Basic Writings,* p. 245.

though Marx's writings assume at many points that man is the subject of historical initiative, he never gives an account of the being of man that clarifies how he can be such a subject. The weight of his effort was directed toward identifying the laws of historical development, the factors that determine the direction of change. As a result, Marxism is characteristically understood as a deterministic system of thought in which everything that happens occurs necessarily and inevitably.[27] In my judgment Garaudy rightly rejects this interpretation of Marx.[28] Marx frequently states that man in any case makes history.[29] The problem is that his acts continually have consequences he neither anticipates nor desires. If he is to act effectively in history, he must have a good grasp of the factors operative in the dynamics of social change. Only by understanding those factors can he utilize them for his own ends. Only by knowing the realistic possibilities for action by means of a critical-empirical analysis of society can he make the active investment of his being count for his own projects.

Still, Marxism is deficient in its failure to show concretely the structures in the being of man that enable him to exercise initiative in relation to the factors that shape and condition his life. Garaudy is sensitive to this deficiency and suggests that the understanding of transcendence in Christian theology can help to overcome it. Transcendence is a category that is usually associated in

[27] Cf. C. Wright Mills' discussion of this point in *The Marxists* (New York: Dell Books, 1962), pp. 91-94.

[28] Roger Garaudy, *Karl Marx: The Evolution of His Thought,* trans. by Nan Aptheker (New York: International Publishers, 1967), pp. 99-109.

[29] Cf., e.g., *Young Marx*, p. 385.

the first instance with the being of God. Yet it always includes a notion of human transcendence as well—man's ability to transcend himself outward in relation to the presence of the transcendent God in human experience. Broadly speaking, the divine transcendence is understood in two fundamentally different ways: (1) the transcendence of that which is eternal and immutable over the transiency and frailty of finite existence, and (2) the transcendence of the future over the limits, even distortions, of the present. In the former, man's capacity for self-transcendence finds expression in his ability to discern and be governed by his intellectual grasp of the eternal and necessary structures of being. It issues in the contemplative life. In the latter, man's ability to transcend himself involves the imaginative projection of a future that surpasses qualitatively the constrictions of the present. It calls forth the active life. It is the latter form of transcendence that is most characteristic of biblical faith. In the words of Karl Rahner, Christianity is the religion of the absolute future.[30] The Christian understanding of transcendence provides a stimulus for the Marxist to explore the way in which man's openness to the future enables him to play a creative role in the historical process. In this frame of reference man is constituted as much by his orientation to new possibilities as by the social and historical factors that shape and condition his being.

Ernst Bloch in particular has furnished significant new insights into the interpretation of man by his reflections on the openness of the future, or, in his terminology, on

[30] "Marxistische Utopie und christliche Zukunft des Menschen," *Der Dialog* (Hamburg: Rowohlt, 1966), pp. 21 ff.

the "principle of hope." Bloch's category of the "not-yet-being" (Noch-Nicht-Sein) points to the creative impact of the pressure of new possibility on the self's concrete struggle to realize itself in relation to the world in which it has its being. It is the promise of the future that enables man to exercise historical initiative in the midst of the world. Bloch's aim is to unite real objective possibilities in the historical process—possibilities that become manifest through a critical-empirical analysis of society—with the unconditional passion for the coming of freedom—a passion that stems from the vision of what is "still not yet." [31]

Both Bloch and Garaudy interpret the promise of the future in a strictly humanistic rather than theistic fashion. They express concern lest Christians fill up the future with God, closing off its openness. Where there is a world ruler, Bloch notes, there is no freedom.[32] He advocates a secularized version of the kingdom of God in which "God" becomes the kingdom of God without God, the messianic openness of the "end-space" that draws man to creative historical activity.[33] In the same vein Garaudy speaks of how the Marxist lives with a "never-satisfied exigency of totality and absoluteness, of omnipotence as to nature and of perfect loving reciprocity of consciousness." [34] He rejects the name of God because it implies a presence, a reality, whereas man lives only toward an exigency, an absence. Nevertheless, both thinkers acknowledge that the sensitivity to the "end-

[31] *Religion im Erbe*, p. 16.
[32] *Ibid.*, p. 142.
[33] *Ibid.*, p. 146.
[34] *From Anathema to Dialogue*, p. 94.

space" or to the "never-satisfied exigency" became an important feature in the consciousness of Western man through the impact of the eschatological expectation of biblical faith.

Garaudy also indicates that Christian theology can deepen the Marxist understanding of subjectivity. This motif is itself connected with the discussion of transcendence, since that discussion is primarily significant for its clarification of how man can be a *subject* of historical initiative, a creator as well as a creature of history. Yet subjectivity also relates to those problems in the struggle for humanness which stem not so much from social factors as from the more intensely personal dimensions of selfhood. Marxism has so emphasized the fact that man is a creature constituted by social relationships that it has tended to assume all human difficulties of any consequence would be removed by a reordering of the structures of society. While no societies embody Marx's hopes for society sufficiently to test his expectations, the experience of socialist societies dramatizes the fact that man's alienation from himself cannot be wholly traced to social factors. Particularly pressing is man's contemporary quest for significant meanings in terms of which he can order and interpret his experience. Issues of this kind have been a major concern of twentieth-century Christian theology and of much contemporary philosophy and literature as well. At this point, therefore, Marxists are open to fresh insights and perspectives on man in his struggles to realize his humanness in the context of modern society.[35]

[35] In addition to acknowledging the prophetic role played by many Christian pastors in social and political struggles, Milan

I have surveyed the major features in the Marxist shift in its attitude toward Christianity, moving from a critical rejection of Christianity, to a realistic acknowledgment of its staying power, to a readiness to learn from it. Similar note must be taken of developments within Christianity that open it to a new relation of dialogue with Marxism.

Christian Openings to Marxism

Generally speaking, Christians have not been as much in agreement in assessing Marxism as Marxists have been in assessing Christianity. Responses have ranged from a bitter denunciation of Marxism as an unmitigated evil to an advocacy of its economic and political tenets as the most adequate expression of the social message of Christianity. This diversity in part reflects variations in the circumstances of the Communist-Christian encounter, but it also indicates that Christians have some unfinished business in seeking to come to terms with the Marxist challenge.

A number of the developments within Christian theology that equip it for dialogue with Marxist thought have no special relation to the Marxist challenge. They are reflections of the more general concern of Christian theologians to interpret Christianity in a manner that is relevant to the contemporary world. For example, any

---

Machovec gives primary emphasis to motifs which might be subsumed under Garaudy's category of subjectivity. Cf. esp. "Der Sinn des menschlichen Lebens," *Disputation,* ed. by M. Stöhr (Munich: Kaiser, 1966), pp. 75-95. See also *Marxismus und Dialektische Theologie,* trans. from the original Czech by D. Neumarker (EVZ-Verlag, Zürich: 1965), pp. 180 ff.

adequate theology for our time must be able to deal openly and creatively with the revolutionary impact of modern scientific thinking on man's intellectual life. It is not sufficient merely to make grudging concessions to scientific advances where concessions are unavoidable, while attempting at the same time to preserve everything else virtually unchanged. What is called for is boldness in reformulating the basic themes of faith in a manner that is compatible with the role scientific thinking currently plays in man's perception of himself and his world. Major Protestant thinkers have for some time been engaged in this undertaking. The extraordinary influence of the efforts of Pierre Teilhard de Chardin to interpret Christian faith in relation to the evolutionary theory of the life sciences suggests a new readiness within Roman Catholicism to respond positively to the scientific consciousness of contemporary man. The continuing vitality of Christianity depends in part upon its ability to clarify its place in a modern, scientific age.

If openness to science is an essential feature of contemporary expressions of Christianity, it is also a necessary part of any fruitful dialogue with Marxist thinkers. Marxism prides itself on its scientific character and condemns the role religion has played in interfering with scientific research and development. Marxists cannot recognize Christians as serious dialogue partners unless a constructive relationship between the life of faith and scientific activity can be established. To be sure, Marxists have themselves distorted the meaning of science, at times claiming scientific proof for views that are in fact based on ideological considerations. Some important Marxist convictions, e.g., the perfectibility of the human spirit or the progressive character of history, are hardly amenable to scientific demonstration at all. Still, Christians cannot effectively challenge the pseudoscience that finds its way into Marxist writings unless it is also prepared to reject the defensiveness that has characterized the history of its own relation to science.

In like manner, recent interpretations of Christianity have given increasing attention to the contributions Christian faith can make to man's quest for fullness of life in *this world*. Otherworldly concerns have diminished in importance, in many cases disappearing altogether. This shift in focus reflects the efforts of Christian theologians to exhibit the significance of faith for modern, secular men. At the same time, it helps to bring about a situation of dialogue with Marxist thinkers. Unlike most secular men, Marxists are not simply uninterested in religious beliefs about the "other" world; they see such beliefs as a positive threat to the humanization of men in this world. Insofar as Christianity maintains its otherworldly hopes, it finds itself challenged to show not only that these hopes do not hinder the worldly progress of the human pilgrimage, but also that they strengthen man in that pilgrimage. Roger Garaudy quotes Teilhard with approval on this point: "In my opinion the world will not be converted to the heavenly promises of Christianity unless Christianity has previously been converted to the promises of the earth." [36]

It must be emphasized that the worldly orientation of Christian theology has been chiefly concentrated on matters that are highly personal, such as death, guilt, or

[36] *From Anathema to Dialogue*, p. 53.

the struggle of each man to make sense of his own life. In their analysis of these matters, Christian theologians have frequently abstracted the being of man from the concrete social, economic, and political factors that shape and condition his life. Dietrich Bonhoeffer has aptly criticized such theology as merely a secularized version of the old pietistic concern for individual salvation in the world to come.[37] With regard to social questions this abstraction has the effect of providing an indirect religious sanction for the status quo. That contemporary Marxist philosophers have become interested in these more personal matters has already been noted. In fact, their readiness to discuss issues such as subjectivity and transcendence may present a temptation to Christian theologians to restrict the agenda of the dialogue to questions with which they are already familiar.[38] Yet Christianity cannot effectively address the situation of contemporary man unless it seeks to come to grips with basic social questions.

The most crucial precondition for Christian openness to dialogue with Marxism is not simply that Christians be oriented to worldly concerns, but that they be committed to explore the meaning of Christian faith in relation to the *social* character of those concerns. It is in regard to these questions that Marxism has made and can continue to make the greatest contribution to the development of Christian thought.

For Christians to become vitally interested in social

[37] *Letters and Papers from Prison* (New York: Macmillan, 1962), pp. 195-96.
[38] Harvey Cox expresses concern over this possibility in "The Christian Marxist Dialogue: What Next?" p. 25.

questions is an important achievement in itself. Yet much is at stake in how these questions are approached. For example, Christian theologians sometimes deal with social questions solely in terms of the *ethical implications* of Christian faith, as if the basic issues of faith were only indirectly related to man's life in society. In contrast Marx located the root of the human problem in a certain ordering of human society and saw the hope of human fulfillment in action aimed at bringing about fundamental changes in that form of social organization. If Marx's thought was too simplistic in linking both man's suffering and his hope to the economic and political structures of human society, Christianity has not given sufficient attention to the way in which the central thrust of the Christian message confronts men in the midst of the social and political struggles of life. Even Reinhold Niebuhr, who has probably done as much as anyone to relate Christian faith to social questions, traced the basic dilemma of man to a highly personalistic source—the anxiety produced by man's finite freedom, by the uneasy union of nature and spirit in his being. Without obscuring the significance of man's personal life, openness to dialogue with Marxism requires Christian theologians to develop the meaning of Christianity's redemptive promise to men in terms of the structures that order men's life in society.

Christian theologians have sometimes dealt with social questions in a purely utopian manner, projecting ideal forms of human social life in the hope that such ideals might lure men to make the needed reforms in society. The social gospel characteristically took this form, failing to appreciate the relative impotence of moral ideals for influencing human behavior. In contrast, Marx sought to gain theoretical competence in the interpretation of the dynamics of social change in order that he might identify effective means for overcoming oppression and exploitation in human society. If the Christian promise is relevant to man's life in society, then Christian theology must also seek to develop or utilize a theoretical understanding of society that can make more effective the concrete efforts of men to give actuality to that promise. Alfred North Whitehead once suggested that Christianity is a religion in search of a metaphysic. In our time it may be more urgent for it to be a religion in search of a social theory, one that will enable it to call men to enter into the redemptive possibilities that are present in the historical process.

A recognition by Christian theologians of the need for a theoretical understanding of social processes inevitably points toward an openness to Marxist thought. Marxism has a number of features that commend it to Christians. For one thing, Marx's serious study of political economy was not motivated by a purely academic interest, but by a concern to bring about humanizing changes in society. In this respect, it has a profoundly moral content. Second, Marx's study embodied a deep emotional identification with the sufferings and needs of oppressed peoples. He was seeking to find means of social change and forms of social organization which at least held the promise of a fundamental alteration in the situation of oppression. His aims must be contrasted with the aims of those who seek only the minimal changes necessary to preserve with some measure of stability the present distribution of power and privilege in society. Marx's central thesis seems to be that there is no way to assure meaningful participation by the masses of people in the determination of their own future unless all men share in the ownership of the means of production. The formal guarantees of freedom provided by the liberal democratic state fail to give adequate protection for the people as long as a minority is able to monopolize the means of production in that society. Christians concerned about human dignity, freedom, and equality of opportunity—not simply as ideals, but as concrete actualities in human life and experience—cannot legitimately disregard the questions Marx raises about the effects economic factors have on the social and political well-being of man.

Through the leadership of Reinhold Niebuhr, disciplined social thinking has in recent decades played a much larger role in American theology than in continental theology. By the mid fifties something of a Christian consensus regarding Marxism had developed in American theology. This consensus was sympathetic, yet critical, toward Marxism. It endorsed the Marxist attack on the exploitation of wage labor in advanced capitalist societies, but denied the contention that the best way to overcome this exploitation is by a proletarian revolution. It appropriated the Marxist concern for the alienation of the human spirit in modern industrial society, but refused to trace that alienation solely to a certain manner of ordering the productive relations of society. In part, it treated alienation as the inescapable accompaniment of modern technology; in part it located the problem of alienation in the finite freedom of the individual, removing it from an exclusive connection with social questions. In like manner, the American consensus about

Marxism conceded an important role to economic factors in determining the course of historical development, but it also emphasized the importance of noneconomic factors—including the value content of human culture—in shaping the quality of human life. Finally, it acknowledged that the Marxist critique of religion had much to commend it, but it denied that this critique provided an adequate interpretation of the significance of religion in the human pilgrimage. Indeed, it contended that communism itself functions as a secular religion in spite of its attempts to dissociate itself from everything religious. Moreover, because it lacks the dimension of transcendence which provides the possibility for radical self-criticism, it is a religion ever subject to the idolatrous perversion of elevating the finite and the relative to a status of ultimacy.[39]

The sharpest criticisms of Marxism in this American "consensus" were directed not against the Marxist analysis of society, but against the Marxist prescriptions for society, especially as these found expression in communist practice. In Niebuhr's writings, these criticisms centered on the moral pretensions of communism.[40] In his view, the primary difficulty with Marxism is that it locates the source of evil exclusively in the structures of society, principally in the relations of production. As a result, one class—the bourgeoisie—is identified as the oppressor class, the sole bearer of social evil, and another class—the proletariat—is identified as the liberator class,

[39] Cf. Reinhold Niebuhr, "The Religion of Communism," *Atlantic Monthly*, CXCVII (Apr., 1931) , 462-70.

[40] Cf. Reinhold Niebuhr, "Can We Avoid Catastrophe?" *Christian Century*, LXV, No. 21 (May 26, 1948) , p. 504.

the sole bearer of the conscience of civilization. In this frame of reference, a just society could presumably be assured by the complete triumph of the proletariat. When a class is viewed as messianic and endowed with every virtue, Niebuhr charged, it is inevitably blind to the moral ambiguities of its own acts. It continually falls prey to a demonic self-righteousness. The dangers of this self-righteousness are intensified by what Niebuhr called the utopian illusions of the communist movement. Utopianism, for Niebuhr, does not mean entertaining in the imagination an impossible ideal as a lure to social progress; it refers to the belief that an ideal society can actually be obtained by revolutionary action. Because the communist movement does not acknowledge the moral contradictions that accompany every level of social advance, but thinks it can bring into being a society that overcomes alienation and oppression, it considers itself fully justified in using any means whatever to realize its own aims, including the repression and destruction of its opponents. Niebuhr notes how this moral pretension further provides a justification for the creation of a monopoly of power, first in a single class, then in a single party, then in a ruling clique within the party, and finally in the tyrannical authority of a single man. Once it is assumed that the true interests of all men are linked with the interests of a single class, then the party that acts for that class or the leadership that guides that party is free to treat any opposition as a deviation from the true good of man and as a threat to the righteous cause that ought to claim all men. For Niebuhr the primary basis of the evil of communism, therefore, is not its lack of moral content, but its pretension to moral virtue, a pretension that obscures the ambiguity of its actions and sanctions a fanaticism that is apt to increase rather than decrease the destructive conflicts among men.

In view of the power and penetration of Niebuhr's analysis, it is not surprising that it gained widespread acceptance in American religious and political thought. Unfortunately, however, it has tended to foreclose fresh considerations of the Marxist challenge, even reinforcing the inclinations in American society to define all issues in terms of an anticommunist crusade. Moreover, Niebuhr's own social thought has become increasingly serviceable in supporting essentially conservative social and political positions. Since all efforts to change society are morally ambiguous, it has been argued, the better part of wisdom is to find realistic ways to work within the established structures of society, hopefully mitigating in some measure its worst features. If the Marxist confidence in the future is subject to utopian illusions, Niebuhr's "realism" is in danger of becoming merely a sophisticated rationalization for the status quo, a handy intellectual tool to defend the interests of privileged persons and groups.

The current stage of the Marxist-Christian dialogue is emerging in a context not significantly influenced by Niebuhr or the consensus which developed around his thought. Theologically, it gives greater weight to the redemptive possibilities of the historical process than to the moral ambiguities of history. Because of this emphasis, it is more able to correct against the opportunistic tendencies of men to accommodate themselves to the injustices of the prevailing society. It frees them to struggle with the destructive features of society, to contradict them, in order that new possibilities might be brought into being. The problem of man's moral pretensions has not been a prominent part of this dialogue, in large measure because the Marxist participants have themselves been more cautious in stating their actual expectations for the future. In any case, Christians cannot respond adequately to the new openings for dialogue with Marxist philosophers unless they are themselves prepared to study social processes with the same depth and intensity that is found in Reinhold Niebuhr's own writings.

Attempts to interpret Christian faith in relation to social processes, particularly those involved in the struggles of oppressed peoples to bring into being a more fulfilling social order, have important implications for theological method. They call into question methodologies that view theology as a self-contained intellectual discipline, perhaps committed to the exegesis of Scripture or to the systematic explication of the meaning of the biblical message for contemporary man. They point instead to a way of doing theology that is shaped and conditioned by the concrete commitment of a community of faith to play a healing, reconciling role in the social and political struggles of men. Biblical exegesis and systematic thinking are not omitted from the latter understanding. Still, they enter most directly into the theological enterprise as activities aimed at helping the struggling community gain insight into the meaning of its own involvements. The crucial tests for this way of doing theology are its power in illuminating the anguish and the promise of the human situation, and its faithfulness in attesting the healing, liberating, and enabling presence of God to men in that situation. Where it does its work well, theology can be the means through which men are empowered to lay hold of the possibilities presented to them for the realization of a new quality of human life.[41]

Theology that follows this "reflection-in-action" model has many affinities with the Marxist view of the relation of thought and being. Marx argued that thought emerges out of the material conditions of life and is shaped by those conditions. Properly used, it is placed in the service of responsible action to master the forces of nature and to change the character of society for the sake of human fulfillment. It is finally tested by its effectiveness in guiding practice. This view of the knowing process is most familiar to Americans through the writings of the philosophical pragmatists—Charles Pierce, William James, and John Dewey. If Christian theology cannot treat thought exclusively as an instrument that enables man to gain mastery over his world, it can properly emphasize the role thought plays in clarifying and attesting man's freedom to work out the meaning of his being in and through his engagement with the actualities of the world. The whole question of an appropriate theological method is one that could be well served by the Marxist-Christian dialogue.

One final matter requires at least brief mention: the meaning of God in human experience. It is well known that Marxism from the beginning has been militantly

[41] Harvey Cox has most effectively argued this point, not only in the *Dialog* article but also in his celebrated *Secular City* (New York: Macmillan, 1965). See esp. the section dealing with the "Anatomy of a Revolutionary Theology," pp. 114-24.

atheistic. Its atheism deserves profound respect, since it
is an atheism "for the sake of man." If Marxism is to be
open to dialogue with Christianity, it must reexamine
the question of God, attending more carefully to what
contemporary theologians mean by God and to the positive possibilities the reality of God brings to human life.
We have seen the readiness of some Marxists to explore
these matters in connection with the notion of transcendence, particularly a transcendence that moves toward
the future. A Christian readiness to dialogue with
Marxists likewise requires an openness to the problematic
nature of belief in God, including its possible demonic
consequences in human experience. Once again, the urgency of this issue in contemporary Christian theology
does not stem solely from the encounter with Marxism,
as the recent "death of God" discussion makes perfectly
clear. Still, this dialogue does provide a context in which
fresh thinking on the meaning of God has begun to
unfold. The important point to be kept in mind is that
the problem of atheism is inherent in the Christian
understanding of God. As Moltmann has so aptly put it,
we must be atheists not simply for the sake of man, but
also for the sake of God.[42] This means that Christian
theology is constantly charged with the task of exposing
false gods—the gods that impoverish and enslave the
being of man. Because of the threats and uncertainties
that assail his being, man is constantly tempted to create
a cosmic excuse upon which he can project his anxieties
and fears and so relieve himself of responsibility for a

[42] *Religion im Erbe,* p. 15. Cf. also Leslie Dewart's analysis of
"relative atheism" in *The Future of Belief* (New York: Herder
and Herder, 1966) , pp. 55-63.

realistic grappling with the limits and possibilities of his own situation. Christian theology must make it unmistakably clear that the god who is an excuse, a barrier to responsibility, is an impostor god from whom man has been liberated. On the other side of this Christian atheism it is called to witness to the God who is present to man not to control him or overpower him, but to liberate him, empower him, and open up new possibilities by means of which man himself can enter into the struggle for the fulfillment of all the promises of God.

The dialogue between Marxists and Christians is only beginning. It is not possible at this time to predict where it will lead, but it promises to make a contribution not only to greater mutual understanding, but also to the continued development and enrichment of both perspectives.

The Revolution of Freedom:
The Christian and Marxist
Struggle

JÜRGEN MOLTMANN
Translated by M. Douglas Meeks

The dialogue between Christians and Marxists in Europe has completely changed during the past few years. Recently, on my way to give lectures in Prague, I bought a copy of *Time* magazine in Frankfort and read the long article on the "God-is-dead movement" in the United States. When I arrived in Prague, a series of articles by the Marxist philosopher Gardavski on Jacob, Jesus, Paul, and Augustine was given to me. The title was: "Buh neni zcela martev"—"God is not quite dead." That is symptomatic of the changing fronts between Christians and Marxists. When the Paulus Society met last year in the Czechoslovakian city of Marienbad, this

realignment was recognized openly.[1] The Christians—
Catholics and Protestants—attempted to demonstrate the
relevance of the Christian faith for this world. They
accentuated the engagement of the church with society,
the hope for the earth, and the necessity of a Christian
critique of unjust social conditions. The Marxists, on
the other hand, revised their well-known "critique of
religion" and asked for a new openness of men for transcendence. It was expected that the theologians would be
assigned the care of transcendence, while the Marxists
would assume responsibility for the formation of this
world in a revolutionary way. However, paradoxically
enough, we found it to be exactly the reverse.

Professor Prucha from Prague, a scholar of the
Lomonossow University of Moskaw, confronted his com-
rades with this query: "Our Christian friends have
awakened in us the courage for transcendence. For a long
time we Marxists have tried to criticize and retard the
Christian striving for transcendence. Should it not rather
be our task to encourage the Christians to be even more
radical in their striving for transcendence?"

Professor Machovec, philosopher of religion in Prague,
supported the view that after the solution of the economic problems, the "search for the meaning of life"
would become more and more the crucial problem of
the future.

Roger Garaudy said to the audience: "What would
your [i.e., the Christian's] faith be like if it bore not in
itself the latent atheism which prevents you from serving

[1] Cf. "Marienbader Protokolle," in *Neues Forum: Zeitschrift
für den Dialog,* Vol. XIV (Vienna, June/July, 1967), 162-63.

a false god? What would our atheism be like if it would not learn from your faith the transcendence of a God of whom we have no living experience?"

Lastly, there was Dr. Gardavski from Brünn, whom I have already mentioned, asking: "Can the Marxian atheist expect of a Christian the same responsibility for the future of mankind as he himself is willing to bear? Can he assume for himself co-responsibility for that idea which is meaningful to Christians, namely, to work for the coming of God's Kingdom?" And he said "yes" to both questions. Due to recent Christian achievements, such as Vatican II, the Encyclical "Populorum Progressio," and the Geneva World Conference on "Church and Society," Christianity looks different to a sensitive Marxist than it did to Karl Marx and Friedrich Engels. On the other hand, Christians also have to acknowledge that Marxism in Europe has changed since the time of Stalin. The humanists lift up their heads. Their Marxism is no longer a dogmatic ideology but a critical philosophy. Under these presuppositions a new dialogue can begin today. For today we are *both* struggling with new problems that were not encompassed in our traditional doctrines.

Some men base their community on answers alone. Such communities are always biased, factious, and confessional. But they cannot be universal. However, there is also a community of men based on asking. This is the community of the seeking and hungry, neither biased nor confessional. It is a community pervading all parties and churches, uniting men in their common experience of deficiency and not-knowing. Such a community of questioning and seeking can today unite Christians and

Marxists. Formerly, the Marxists appeared to us as dogmatists who had the right answer to all questions. Today, Christian theologians appear to be possessors of an unquestionable and incontrovertible truth. Often they have answers to all human questions and are astonished that people are unwilling to pose questions to them any more. Bertolt Brecht once wrote a nice almanac story: "I have noticed," said Mr. Keuner, "that we scare away many people from our doctrine because we know an answer to everything. Couldn't we, in the interest of our propaganda, comprise a list of questions which seem to us to be completely unsolved?"

It seems to me that Christian theology of today should turn away from a dogmatic theology to a critical one, from beginning with answers about God to the unsolved asking for God. The tense of asking is the future. In the process of asking persistently and eschewing the satisfaction of trite compensations, man becomes open to the future and thus exists in time and history.

By way of asking he goes, as Abraham once did, from his country and his kindred and his father's house. By way of asking he opens himself up for the unknown future. By way of asking for God and ultimate freedom he enters into worldwide solidarity with the whole "waiting creation" of which Paul speaks in Romans 8:18 ff. A "theology of hope" is a theology of questions that can be answered only by the coming of God through the kingdom of his freedom. It can, therefore, be ecumenical if, behind the conflict between the different answers of the churches and ideologies, it detects and brings to awareness the deeper community of asking and seeking, a community bonded by man's poverty and existing for the sake of a wider future.

I shall now attempt to outline some of the characteristic points of a theology of freedom as it is possible in the new dialogue between Christians and Marxists, Liberals and Socialists.

The Religion of Freedom [2]

The Christian faith understands itself authentically as the beginning of a freedom that was, hitherto, unseen to the world (John 1:18; I Cor. 2:9). Christian faith not only believes in freedom but is already freedom itself. It not only hopes for freedom, but rather is in itself the inauguration of a free life on earth. However, it is only a historical beginning and not yet the universal fulfillment.

There is a fundamental difference between the "realm of freedom," which we hope will ultimately free the whole creation from its misery, and the beginning of freedom here in the midst of a world full of bondage and slavery. Christian faith is freedom in struggle, in contradiction, and in temptation. The realm of freedom, however, of which the present beginning is faith, is freedom in its own new world—that is, God's free world. The difference between freedom in faith and the realm of freedom is the motor and the motive power for our work of realizing freedom in history.

Is Christianity a religion of freedom? At the starting point of biblical faith, we see the creative symbols of

[2] Cf. my article, "Die Revolution der Freiheit," in *Evangelische Theologie,* Vol. 27, no. 11 (1967), pp. 595-616.

freedom: the Exodus of Israel from bondage in Egypt, and the resurrection of the crucified Christ into the coming kingdom of God—a deliverance *in* history and a deliverance *from* history.

The future for which Christian faith is hoping is a new creation in which the whole groaning creation shall be set free from the bondage of evil and death. Christians who believe in God believe in the coming, creative God, who will create out of the misery of the living creatures the kingdom of his glory, a new being in which he himself will dwell. In their faith, Christians participate in the creative freedom of God. Thus, faith should no longer be described in the terms of Schleiermacher only as a *schlechthinninges Abhängigkeitsgefühl*—i.e., as the "feeling of absolute dependence" in religious submissiveness. Faith can, on the contrary, be described as a *schlechthinninges Freiheitsgefühl,* as the "feeling of absolute freedom" in the spiritual communion with the creative God. As the Gospel puts it: "All things are possible to him who believes" (Mark 9:23 RSV) ; "with God all things are possible" (Matthew 19:26 RSV). "For all things are yours, whether . . . the world or life or death or the present or the future, all are yours; and you are Christ's; and Christ is God's," proclaims the apostle Paul (I Cor. 3:21-23) . Thus, Christian proclamation is actually the religion of an exceedingly great freedom, even though the Christian church has often concerned itself more with authority and order than with this freedom.

This freedom in faith must be made clear to the atheist as well as to the religious man of today, for he is still thinking: Either there is a God, then man cannot be free; or man is free, then there cannot or may not be a God (cf. Marx, Engels, Bakunin, Sartre, N. Hartmann, and others). Those are actually the alternatives in the mythological world of religions. For in that world the half-god Prometheus becomes the hero of man's freedom over against the gods. He is still the philosophical saint of Marxism. Here, God and man are considered to be of one and the same essence. Thus, what you grant God, you must have taken away from man, and what you grant to man, you must have taken away from God. But when will we stop measuring God and man with the same yardstick?

In the Old Testament, however, things are different. Jahweh is here the God who leads his people out of the house of bondage. Thus he is the God of freedom, the God ahead of us. One acquires social, political, and world-surpassing freedom from God, not against him.

In the New Testament, Jesus is believed in as the Messiah of freedom because he sets sinners free through his word and liberates the sick by his wondrous works. Those who labor and are heavy laden, the humiliated and offended, the poor and hungry find freedom and justice in him. In his resurrection from death on the cross we can see freedom dawn, freedom from the power of death and from the misery of the eclipse of God. In Jesus we can see the Messiah of God's freedom on earth. For he did not seek to be master of mankind but took the form of a servant. His suffering works as the unburdening of man in order to set man free. For freedom is always born out of unburdening. Freedom of faith is born out of his serving, joy out of his suffering, life everlasting out of his death. Kings and emperors have called themselves God's representatives on earth, founding their authority in the supreme authority of God. However, if we believe the crucified Christ to be the representative of God on earth, we see the glory of God no longer in the crowns of the mighty but in the face of that man who was executed on the gallows. What the authorities intended to be the greatest humiliation—namely, the cross—is thus transformed into the highest dignity. It follows that the freedom of God comes to earth not through crowns—that is to say, through the struggle for power—but through love and solidarity with the powerless.

Therefore, in spite of Romans 13, Christians are hoping for a future in which "every rule, every authority and power" will be destroyed (I Cor. 15:24) and the crucified shall reign, "the first among many brethren." Already here in history, they will strive for neutralizing and destroying the differences between the powerful and the powerless, master and slave. The community comprised of Jews and heathen, of masters and slaves, becomes the prototype and sacrament of men's hope for a world of brotherhood (I Cor. 1:20-29).

Therefore, Christian freedom is not a special one, different from that freedom for which all mankind is longing. Nor is it a partial one that is exhausted in the practice of a certain religion or cult. If it really is the beginning of the realm of freedom in the midst of all the misery of this world, then Christians can only demonstrate this freedom by using their own freedom for the actual liberation of man from his real misery. Privileges are always the perversion of freedom. If religion induces not new freedom *for* the world but only new chains, then

—according to the word of Karl Marx—the liberation *from* religion would bring about more freedom than would religious liberty.

Which aspects of concrete freedom do Christians claim for themselves? They do not seek the liberties of liberalism, in which each one may go to heaven according to his own fashion if only he does not impede the fashion of others.

Freedom is no private affair, but is always freedom *for* others. Therefore, the Christian faith cannot acquiesce in the liberties of individual people. To believe is no private hobby, but hope for the whole, for society, for mankind, for the earth. On the other hand, socialism cannot be the heir of Christian freedom, for neither a social nor a political system of life is able to realize already, here and now, that future of freedom for which the Christian faith hopes. The Christian faith will find its peace only when it rests in the realm of God's freedom. Until then, however, it remains a troublemaker in every society that is content with itself and coerces its people to regard themselves as happy and fortunate. Thus Christians must seek the freedom for their own original mission in every form of society. Specifically, they must search for (1) the freedom of proclaiming God's liberating power publicly, (2) the freedom of assembling a new congregation of brothers out of Jews and heathen, masters and slaves, black and white, (3) the freedom of critically cooperating in the process of community according to the criteria of creative love. But Christians will also always seek for possibilities of working together with Liberals, Democrats, and Marxists for the sake of the realm of freedom. For the hope for an all-embracing and ultimate freedom and the belief in a creative future have inspired all our freedom movements. But in none of them has it been materialized until now, for every revolution for freedom has evolved new unfreedom in the world, too. Let us now survey briefly the history of the revolutions for freedom.

The History of Revolutions for Freedom

All those whose struggle for freedom commits them to participation in dialogue—namely Catholics, Protestants, Liberals, and Communists—are rooted in particular historical revolutionary freedom movements. Therefore, they understand freedom differently. But since all of them stand in one and the same history in which people have searched for freedom, they find a deep community existing among themselves.

Today the Marxists criticize Christianity by pointing to a historical distinction. For them the history of Christianity is the continuous conflict between a Constantinian wing, in which the state church is linked with the ruling powers, and a chiliastic wing which is united with the humiliated and oppressed in a revolutionary way. This distinction is correct to a large degree. But it flings back to the Marxists like a boomerang, for we must equally distinguish between a Stalinistic Marxism, showing the symptoms of a byzantine or bureaucratic state ideology, and a humanistic Marxism, which is, in a self-critical way, allied with those who are humiliated and disappointed in socialist countries as well. These mutual self-distinctions are very helpful, for they indicate that in our present day the front in the struggle for freedom runs right through the churches and parties. The nonconformists of all countries and parties recognize each other in order possibly to form a new alliance. But the history of freedom reaches further, as one may suppose, than these very important alternatives.[3]

Freedom out of Christ

When the Christian faith came into being in the ancient world, a new kind of man was born. For him the act of existing no longer meant entering into a relationship with the eternal rules of polis and cosmos, but now meant to be set free through Christ for a life of free decisions. Thus, life in history was made meaningful for the first time. The past was considered as the power of sin, the future as the dynamic of grace, and the present became the time of decision.[4] This was the pattern of the Christians' struggle against the idolatry of nature, of fate, and of political power. Christians did away with the idolatry of nature because they believed in God the Creator. They did away with the idolatry of fate in history because they hoped for the kingdom of freedom. They demythologized the cult of Caesar because they worshiped God in the name of the Crucified. Christianity always took a stand for the coming theocracy of freedom;

[3] Cf. Eugen Rosenstock-Huessy, *Die europäischen Revolutionen und der Charakter der Nationen,* 3rd ed., 1951.

[4] Cf. Rudolf Bultmann, *Theology of the New Testament* (New York: Scribner's, 1961), chaps. 38-40.

otherwise it would not have been persecuted. Christianity was thus to some extent historically justified in participating in the Constantinian effort to Christianize the world of that time, for Christians considered Constantine to be the emperor of peace over the expected kingdom of freedom (Eusebius of Caesarea). However, out of this realization of freedom there grew, at the same time, its well-known disappointment. Out of this situation was born the next task in the history of freedom: the liberation of the church from the power of a Christian Caesar.

The Freedom of the Church

The spell of the Constantinian age—that is, Christian faith in terms of the ancient Roman religion—did not break until the great revolution of the papacy and the church reform of Cluny in the Middle Ages. In the struggle between Pope and Caesar concerning "Ecclesiastical Investiture" the church recovered her autonomy and, thus, the possibility of acting freely. But there was more in it than meets the eye: The kingdom of God on earth was now embodied in the power of the keys of the Pope and the church, rather than in the government of an anointed Christian Caesar. *Libertas Ecclesiae* became the slogan for the "realm of freedom" in the Middle Ages. However, this new Christian freedom had its price—namely, the clericalization of the church. Clericalization marked a bad consequence of the magnificent liberation of the church from the emperor. Everybody could see that this church was not yet the "realm of freedom" itself.

The Freedom of a Christian Man

The Reformation was not simply a protest against the clericalization of the Christian freedom. Here the birth of a new kind of man took place once again. According to Luther's treatise, "The Freedom of a Christian" (1520), and Calvin's chapter on *"de libertate Christiana" (Institutes* III, 19), freedom is born out of the justifying gospel in everyone who believes. If Christ himself is the ground of freedom in everyone's life, everyone becomes "a perfectly free lord of all, subject to none." However, if the ground of this freedom lies in the crucified Christ, every believer voluntarily becomes "a perfectly dutiful servant of all, subject to all." In the congregation of brotherhood without hierarchy everyone becomes "Christ" to his fellowman. The privileges of the clergy are liquidated for the sake of the "common priesthood of all believers." Every worldly work is understood to be a divine calling into the liberation of the world from the realm of Satan:

The reformation of the Christian freedom, however, brought forth its perversions, too. The redresses of the princes and landed nobles who truly loved to fight for *religio et libertas* finally developed into a Protestant form of Constantinianism, a new particular religion of the national well-being, oppressing the enthusiastic wing of the reformation and dividing the unity of the church. And here can be found the origin of the well-known resignation on the Continent which no longer seeks the kingdom of God and man's freedom outwardly in social and political change, but inwardly alone, deep in the ground of the individual's soul.

These new chains of freedom were effectively broken first by West European reformations. In the name of the common "kinghood of all believers" Calvinism struggled against the absolutist sovereigns. In the struggle for freedom of conscience the state was neutralized in England. The Presbyterians succeeded in establishing the right of free congregations against the state church. The Congregation consists of free people who are all born to be rulers, not slaves, because they all exist in the image of God, said John Milton. Therefore, the crown rests upon the democratic constitution of the free and not upon the head of a single person. The freedom of the image of God was thus maintained over against the sinful supremacy of men over men. The perversions of this freedom movement originated from the fact that freedom and the right of lifting up one's head were limited to the "Christian man." This is the reason why this movement was soon taken over and surpassed by the humanism of the Enlightenment, for the realm of freedom is characterized by universality and breaks up all limitations and barriers created by man.

The Freedom of the Citizen

In the definition of human rights in America and France, freedom finally becomes a secular phenomenon. Man is born free. This freedom of man is not to be denied or abandoned. It has to be the irreducible basis of civil rights in society. Everybody has the right to determine freely and to seek his fortune and happiness as long as he respects the same freedom of others. Therefore, everybody has the right to criticize all kinds of "happiness" imposed on him from above or by other people. These personal liberties are unforgettable once they are articulated. The free development of the humane in every single person is the presupposition of the humanization of society. But these liberties have also brought forth their inevitable disappointments. There was, first, the disillusionment of the French Revolution. People had stormed the barricades for the sake of "human rights," with the despicable result that political rights were disposed of by the propertied citizens. On the other side, there is the general misery of the bourgeois society, which "does not permit man to find the realization but rather the barrier of his freedom in the other person," as Karl Marx rightly pointed out.[5]

The Socialism of Freedom

The civil revolution had not done away with the difference between "man" and "citizen." This became the starting point for the next, the socialist revolution, which wants to liberate men from economic slavery. Its way, thus, leads from the propertied bourgeois society and its private men to socialism and its "men in society." From the political emancipation of men it turns to the social emancipation of men, from which the "human emancipation of every person" is expected—"an association, in which the free development of every person implies the free development of all men" (*The Communist Manifesto*). This represents a change from the *society of having* to a society of authentic human *being*.

[5] Karl Marx, *Frühschriften*, Landshut edition (1953), p. 193.

The starting point of this socialist revolution lies in the disillusionary experiences of the French and capitalistic revolutions. Its goal of making man free from his economic misery is a new and significant step toward the universal and eschatological hope of freedom for the whole suffering creation, which is the Christian hope for the salvation of the body.

Nonetheless, this movement of freedom has its perversions, too, and has also added its own chapter to the history of the disappointment of mankind. This disappointing experience is not simply represented by Stalinism, which is horrible to many people. It lies rather in the foreboding that the expected "human emancipation of man" will not come automatically when the economic liberation of men in the socialist industrial states has taken place. This disappointment will certainly become the motor of post-Marxist revolutions. The relation between the "realm of freedom" and the "realm of work" remains ambiguous even in Karl Marx. On the one hand, he describes the "Kingdom of freedom" as a sudden transition or change of quantity into new quality. Then the realm of freedom suspends all labor, changing all work into absolutely free "self-activity." "In a communist society, there will no longer be any painters but, at most, people who among other things, like to paint," he says in his early writings.[6] On the other hand, in his later writings Marx described the "realm of freedom" as the outcome of the "realm of work." If this is the case, however, the "realm of freedom" will be forever combined with the "realm of work"

[6] *Ibid.*, p. 475.

and can move forward only in the leisure hours of men guaranteed by automation and the shortening of working hours. Everybody knows, however, that a man with more leisure time does not necessarily become a free man. "Should it be the effect of the great revolution that the number of French sportsmen and anglers is being enlarged?" Jules Romain asked rightly. Consequently, we must make clear whether and how men may become children of freedom so that they may engage in free work. Are we, here and now, children of freedom, or is freedom the reward of our good deeds? If freedom is nothing more than the reward for or success of our deeds, then men will always remain unfree. That is the question of the Reformation to Marxism. That is the question of the freedom through faith to the modern form of justification by works.

The disappointment that in the last analysis Marxism has only advanced industrialization without bringing about the longed-for humanization frustrates the young working people of today in the East, just as competition frustrates their counterparts in the West. The disappointment that the demanded "abolition of the state" has only strengthened the bureaucracy of the ruling elite is today also agonizing Marxists. "In the citizen of the French Revolution the bourgeois was hidden. God have mercy on us, what may be hidden in the comrade," said the Marxist Ernst Bloch in 1930.[7] In struggling against the freedom of competition in the capitalist society, Karl Marx is, in a deeply Christian sense, right when he says that true freedom means "for you to have been the

[7] Bloch, in *Spuren* (1930), p. 32.

mediator between yourself and the species, so as to be known and experienced in yourself as a completion of your own essence and as a necessary part of yourself and therefore to know me confirmed in your thought as well as your love." [8] But what is the "true essence of the species of men," and which group is authorized to determine it? Did not certain groups in society use such collective categories as the "true essence of the human species" and the "universal moral code" in order to mask their claims on power? Truly, it is contradictory to the freedom of man to be made happy from above and to be put under categories of his essence represented by a party or a church. That is contradictory to his history, which is open to the future. Isn't there also a personal freedom of man, which is not the freedom of profitmaking wolves but which presupposes human progress in science and culture? Today we find exactly these basic ideas of a liberal socialism in the Polish Marxists Adam Schaff and Leszew Kolakowski: It is impossible to make people happy by force. But you can eliminate the enormous causes of misfortune (A. Schaff). [9] Whoever defends per-

[8] Marx, MEGA, Vol. I, no. 3, p. 546.

[9] Adam Schaff, *Marxismus und das menschliche Individuum* (1965), p. 236: "If one begins to construct definitions of happiness and to derive out of them obligatory norms of conduct for man— naturally for his own welfare!—then even in socialism the danger of 'making men happy' 'from above' can suddenly emerge. The attempt to make men happy through coercion and according to the currently accepted models of happiness can become the cause of an enormous unhappiness . . . Since there is not such a thing as a happiness which applies to all, one should not seek to create a uniform model of a happy life for all." The real foundation for the activity directed toward human happiness lies not in the

sonal freedom defends human progress (Kolakowski).

Integration of Freedom Movements

The freedom movements based on Christian faith, on the church, on the conscience, on the citizen and socialism have succeeded one another in such a way that the one caught fire in the disappointing consequences of the preceding one as each strove for greater freedom. So far, no one of them has brought about the "realm of freedom" itself, but each one has opened a new front in the struggle for freedom. None of these revolutions was as yet the "last battle," although everyone set out under this apocalyptic sign, be it the struggle against Antichrist, against the beast coming out of the "bottomless pit" (Rev. 17:8), or against the class enemy. Therefore, these movements have always corrected each other. The older brother on the road to freedom must warn his younger brother lest he give up liberties already won for the sake of a new one.

A revolution has to assimilate the tradition of the former revolution, otherwise it achieves not more freedom but simply another liberty. On the other hand, tradition must adapt itself to revolution, otherwise it will not prevail over its own disappointments. Such an integration of Catholics, Protestants, Liberals, and Marxists is possible once all of them learn to look beyond their own systems toward the future of the realm of freedom.

---

understanding "that we make men happy but that we eliminate the exceedingly offensive causes of his unhappiness."

OPENINGS FOR MARXIST-CHRISTIAN DIALOGUE

The Realm of Freedom

Up to now, Christians and Marxists have been involved in a struggle of different ideological positions that excluded and limited each other. Today we have come "de l'anatheme au dialogue" (*From Anathema to Dialogue: A Marxist Challenge to the Christian Churches,* R. Garaudy). We are criticizing each other in order to help each other to realize the best of both our positions. We shall be able to go beyond the dialogue toward cooperation if both sides comprehend that they do not have "positions" or "standpoints," but are rather ways directed toward a yet unknown human future. In many respects these ways could run parallel and supplement each other. In the first place, it is common to Christians and Marxists to suffer under the real misery of mankind. This suffering is always the negative form of hope for the future of men. The Marxists see the misery of man represented in his political dependence, in his economic slavery, and in his being tied up with nature and fate. Thus, freedom implies to their understanding the abolition of the dominion of men over men, the ending of exploitation of men by men, and, finally, the exaltation of a united mankind in which man will be the creator of his own history.

Christians understand that the misery of men lies not simply in their not yet realized possibilities, but even deeper in man's real impossibilities or his lost possibilities. He is enslaved under the dominion of sin, that is, the failure of life because of selfishness and fear. He is handed over to death, transitoriness, and nothingness. Finally, he is exploited by law, which commands him to live in freedom without giving it to him. Hence, freedom implies to Christians the liberation from the curse of the evil deed through grace; it implies freedom from death and fear through hope in the coming God, and freedom from the law of works through faith.

When we compare both sides we do not find them simply opposing each other. What Christians call the misery of man includes, by all means, political, social, and natural misery, and does not exclude these forms as *Christianity Today* does: "Man's problem lies in his sins against the creator, not in domination by capitalistic economic forces." [10] The real possibilities after which Marxists are striving to overcome this misery are also possibilities for the Christians' struggle for freedom.

Nevertheless, the two sides are not exactly identical. Wherever freedom from misery and inhumanity can really be achieved, socially and politically, there Christians discover the immanence of their hope. But wherever in the necessary struggle against evil in the world new dependencies are being produced, there Marxists discover the transcendence of hope. For the realm of freedom is always more than the fragments of a free life which we may accomplish in history. Immanence and transcendence of freedom are not divided dichotomously into two realms, like earth and heaven; rather they form dialectically two aspects of its history. The immanent significance of hope for salvation is visible wherever the emancipation of men from the chains of slavery takes place *in* history. On the other hand, hope for salvation out of this hostile world *of* history is the transcendence

[10] "The Danger of Christian-Marxist Dialogue," in *Christianity Today*, Vol. XII, no. 2 (Oct. 27, 1967) , p. 27.

of all attempts to make this world the homeland for all people. If we conceive that salvation be the transcendence for the immanent emancipation movement of men, then the Christians' "beyond" is not a compensation or "the opium for the people" anymore, but is the power and the ferment of emancipation here and now. Traditionally we have always combined reconciliation with God with the conservation of the earth. But there is no reconciliation without transformation—that is, without personal repentance and social revolution.

Since Feuerbach and Marx, Christians and Marxists have readily "divvied up" "heaven" and "earth." Heinrich Heine mused: "We relinquish heaven to the angels and the birds."

Today we find an attempt to combine both again. Marxists are pleased to quote the sentence of Teilhard de Chardin: "The world will not be converted to the heavenly promise of Christianity unless Christianity has previously been converted to the promise of the earth." On the other hand, theologians are delighted when Roger Garaudy says: "The Christian can open the Marxist to the idea of transcendence."

I think we can overcome this kind of division and combination if we begin to take notice of the eschatological category *novum*. Why do Christians seek their salvation in heaven, and why do they feel redeemed by heavenly promises, if the first heaven will pass away and be replaced by a new heaven? (Rev. 21:1.) Even the Christians will not be "in heaven" safe from the future of the God who judges and creates everything anew. On the other hand, one can ask why the Marxists seek their salvation on the earth and feel secure in earthly promises, if it may be likewise true that "this" earth does not endure but will pass away. Neither heaven nor earth, neither history nor transcendence are, in the last analysis, secure places. There is salvation only in the new creation of heaven and earth, history and transcendence. The "powers of the future world" are historically effective in the "criticism of heaven" just as in the "criticism of earth," i.e., in the liberation from religious and ideological superstition as well as in the liberation from the anonymous and repressive powers of society and from the obstinacy of human work.

We need this power of the new and of the future in order to act with certainty in the midst of the ambiguities of history and of human activity, even our own. All struggles for freedom are ambivalent: How can alienated people struggle against alienation without, in their struggle, producing new alienations? That is the question for the Marxists who see the guilt of Stalinism. How can sinners struggle against sin without producing new sins? That is the question for the Christians who suffer under the guilt of the church. How can the kingdom of nonviolent brotherhood be won without using violence? That is the open question on both sides. For the most part, moral and revolutionary enthusiasm has overlooked this "cross of reality" (Hegel). Therefore, enthusiasm turns into resignation so quickly. By believing only in the "hereafter" the church has tried to view this cross of history as a tragic "vale of tears." In this posture, it was simply waiting for a far-off salvation, while in the meantime stabilizing conservative and repressive powers. Both ways of thinking are one-sided. Revolution of freedom is alive where people hear the categorical imperative "to overthrow all circumstances in which man is a humiliated, subjugated, forsaken, and despicable being." Karl Marx is completely right in this. And if his critique of religion ends with this categorical or eschatological imperative, it is better than all demythologizing of Christianity by theologians too well adjusted to the social, economic, and political status quo. This revolution of freedom, however, attains its end only if we find the certitude that future and freedom do indeed gracefully meet us in our revolutionary struggle.

While Bertolt Brecht was in exile during the Third Reich he wrote his most thoughtful poem. It says:

We who wished to prepare the soil for kindness could not be kind ourselves.
But you, when at last it will come to pass that man is a helper to man, remember us with forbearance.

In a secular way, he has taken up what the continuous plea for reconciliation means to the Christian faith.

It is time now for all the different freedom movements to cooperate in a brotherly way, for the misery of mankind has not become less urgent. The disappointments are growing.

I think it is impossible to reduce Christianity and Marxism, with their divergent positive conceptions, to a lowest common denominator. But a Christian-Marxist cooperation in the present necessary negation of the negative is indeed quite conceivable. In the first place there can be created a common future only out of the common averting of common threats by evil, such as atomic war, catastrophes of famine, and so forth. This method has the advantages (1) of solidarizing very different men and groups, and (2) of leaving open to them the freedom of shaping their own future. We may not know what true humanity is and how a just order of the world looks. But what mankind should not be and which order of things is false we can know by consideration of the past and also by consideration of the future's possible development. Only in the concrete negation of the negative is the other, the positive, open to us. *Solidarity* in suffering and in struggling against evil, *liberality* in goods of the positive, and the *future* belong inexorably together.

None of the mentioned freedom movements has already brought freedom itself, but we find roads leading to its future in all of them. The realm of freedom is greater than all of them. It inspires all our endeavors, but it also condemns all our presumptions and comforts us where we become guilty. At all frontiers of life the summons of the prophet Isaiah is to be heard—"to bind up the brokenhearted, to proclaim liberty to the captives" (Isa. 61:1)—for these are the opportunities of the messianic age, in which, because Christ is born, we live.

Act and Being in Christian
and Marxist Perspective

CHARLES C. WEST

Let me start with a thesis. That Christian-Communist dialogue is emerging today in a new way is well known. It is less noticed that ideologies in general that have in the past been instruments of conflict are learning to interact. But this whole development is set within a social movement whose direction is not toward reconciliation but toward conflict, and it is this fact which calls it in question. In its subjective spirit this movement may be called revolt; in its expressions of political power, revolution.

What is revolution? "L'homme révolté" is, as Albert Camus has shown, an age-old experience of the human race.[1] We may or may not follow Camus in his conviction that man becomes human in the act of saying "no" to the whole enslaving structure of being that had defined his existence before, but the reality to which he points is undeniable. It finds eloquent expression in the exodus of the Jewish people from Egypt. Its biblical roots are probably the earliest in recorded literature. Arnold Toynbee discovers it as the internal proletariat in every great civilization in process of disintegration— that mass of people who lose their sense of identity with the society that the dominant minority rules, who no longer have a stake in it and who express their alienation by finding a focus of their existence outside it. Objectively it is the condition of growing insecurity. Old structures of society give way to new pressures, but the new forces do not provide the means for realizing the hopes they release. Family and communal order breaks down. Wealth and power are centralized. The cities, symbols of new forces of production, trade, and commerce, attract masses who have no roots. Life for these masses becomes ever less tolerable and ever more endangered. But the growth of insecurity and misery is not enough itself to produce revolt and revolution. Subjectively, revolt is based in the growing consciousness that this state of affairs is avoidable, and that therefore it is wrong, dehumanizing, and contrary to the true and proper order of things. The new vision of human possibilities that is released by the accomplishments of the newly rich and powerful, and the religious and philosophical justifications they give of their wealth and

[1] Camus, *The Rebel* (New York: Knopf, 1952) .

position, shed a glaring light on the growing contrast between them and the proletariat they are creating. As a result of both these influences—growing insecurity and rising expectations—the force is created that works for basic overthrow of the powers that be and the structures that sustain them, in the hope of a new and more human world to come.

Thus revolution's age-old characteristics. The task of this essay is to explore the role of Marxism and Christianity in revolution, and their interaction with special reference to a particular issue—the way in which objective reality is conceived and responded to. For both of them have not only focused but intensified the revolutionary experience of man.

I turn first to Karl Marx. It is no accident that the very idea of revolution is today so often associated with his name. In a special way he was the prophet, the ideologue, of the revolutionary consciousness. It was he who brought together the ideology of humanism and the proletarian experience that had gone before him, and provided for modern revolutionary humanists their point of departure and their continuing standard of reference to which they return for inspiration and new direction. Let us look in turn at the two sides of this combination.

First, Karl Marx was a humanist in the full sense of that Renaissance and Enlightenment word. Indeed his philosophy might be called humanism's richest autumn fruit, swollen with all the promises of the untrammeled human spirit, free from every authority to create its own future, and ripened by the sharp, cold frost of emancipated man's doubts and fears about the world he himself was making. He wrote in the preface to his doctoral dissertation at the age of twenty-one:

Philosophy, so long as a drop of blood surges in its world storming heart, will ever cry out to its opponents with Epicurus: "They are not impious who destroy the gods of the multitude, but they who impose upon the gods the beliefs of the multitude." Philosophy does not conceal it. The confession of Prometheus: "In one round sentence, I hate all the gods," is its own confession against all the gods in heaven and on earth who do not acknowledge the human self-consciousness as the highest deity. No other may stand beside him.

In this manifesto Marx was declaring his independence from the prevailing Hegelian spirit of his time. He had chosen to write on the ancient Epicurean philosophy of nature in hopes of finding there, via materialism, that freedom for the human mind which Hegel's synthesis of World Spirit and human spirit seemed always to be denying him. But more deeply he was expressing a spirit profoundly in continuity with Hegel—the spirit of a humanist revolt that had begun more than three centuries before in the art of the Renaissance and had grown through the philosophy of Descartes and the politics of the French Revolution. The heart to this revolt is the confidence that man shall fulfill his own nature and master the world with his own free reason and conscience. It was a revolt against the whole idea of an alien world controlled by a power who is not man, whose will and being one must seek to be secure in life and death. In short, it was a revolt against religion, in the name of the emancipation of man.

The paradox of this development will be immediately

apparent to Christians. The original inspiration for this revolt was, as we shall show more fully below, the biblical Christ himself. Marx and his precedessors, the *philosophes* of eighteenth-century France, made a great deal of the autonomous sovereign human being in the political and philosophical life of ancient Greece. But Greek humanism, as Marx himself came later to see, was limited and, in the long run, defeatist. Its roots were in a slave society that dehumanized the majority. Prometheus, the symbol for these latter-day classicists of unlimited creative power, was in the Greek legends only a titan, not a god, the subordinate pole in an eternal tension with the principle of law and order, Zeus. Rather, the "Prometheanism" of the great humanists of whom Marx was the crown was rooted in the experience of the Apostle Paul:

To me, though I am the very least of all the saints, this grace was given, to proclaim to the nations the unsearchable riches of Christ, and to make all men see what is the economy of the mystery hidden for ages in God who created all things; that through the church the manifold wisdom of God might now be made known to the principalities and powers in the heavenly places. (Eph. 3:8-10)

The dynamic center of reality itself, "the mystery hidden for ages in God," is revealed in the unsearchable riches of Christ, and man is caught up in the total economy of this movement which will subdue all powers and principalities and embrace the nations. Paul himself speaks of having been given an "economy of God's grace" (v. 2).

This dynamic openness of human possibilities by participation in the work of Christ was given expression by the Renaissance, only to clash with the sacred institutions that claimed to define and limit this dynamic. Marx was the end product of a long development whereby in this conflict faith in the second person of the Trinity, in Christ and his work, was torn apart from faith in God. Thus God became the symbol for an order like that of Zeus, increasingly problematic because of the very dynamic of the Christian gospel itself, while man, deprived of the inspiration and promise of Christ, redefined himself in his own drive to dominate and create.

The death of such a God was inevitable, and the Marxists have correctly judged that Hegel was the final executioner. He was so, precisely as a philosophical theologian who was profoundly aware of the internal problems of humanism itself, and who developed theology into a comprehensive metaphysical and mythical system to solve these problems. The goal that Hegel set himself early in his life, and that, despite ambiguity, he never later abandoned, was to expound and promote the apotheosis of man. "The self-elevation of man—from finite life to infinite life," he wrote in an early fragment, "is religion." [2] The aim of life is higher than any definable goal. It is also more than mystical union with God, or the Aristotelian ideal of perfect contemplation of him. It is dynamic spiritualization which conquers every object, the universalization of the self by incorporating all knowledge and power, that Hegel suggests in the dialectical struggle of the human spirit to realize his unity with the World Spirit. Hegel, says Robert Tucker, "was

[2] "Fragment of a System," in *Early Theological Writings,* trans. by T. M. Knox (Chicago: University of Chicago Press, 1948), p. 311. The concept is developed in Hegel's *Philosophy of Religion,* Part II.

engaged in a war of the self similar to the one represented in Kantian philosophy, save that in Hegel the urge to be godlike expressed itself in a quest, not for moral holiness, but for omniscience, absolute knowledge." [3]

Already at this point—as the left Hegelians, Marx among them, were quick to point out—an atheistic interpretation of this dialectic brings out its inner meaning. "God" is the symbol for the absolute, total self-realization and mastery over his environment that man seeks to achieve. The process is immanent. Transcendence is basically mystification. But this religion has an obverse that is equally convincing—atheism. The leading French Marxist philosopher Roger Garaudy published a scholarly study of Hegel—before the modern "death of God" theology came in vogue—under the title, *Dieu est Mort.* The term refers to the dying of Christ. Man, says Hegel, is divine by nature, created to be a creator himself, like God. But he lives his life in self-alienation. He incorporates his humanity in the absolute monarch, who becomes his oppressor, or even in God, who appears as his enemy. He finds himself the victim of the nature that he should be dominating and recreating by his own spirit. The incarnation and sacrifice of Christ is the way by which the division between the finite and the infinite, the divine and the human, is overcome. In him man becomes aware of his true divinity, for in him the worst of human alienation is related to absolute transcendence and liberation. "In accepting the law of birth, which is at the same time that of suffering and death, and in dying the death of the cross, the vilest death of criminals

[3] *Philosophy and Myth in Karl Marx* (Toronto: Macmillan, 1961), p. 42.

(Jesus) bears witness that the most ignoble is at the same time the most noble." This is absolute love. In Hegel's own words, quoted by Garaudy, "One only has the perfect, temporal intuition of the Divine Idea in the present in the death of Christ. The supreme alienation of the divine Idea: God is dead, God himself is dead, is a tremendous, terrible, vicarious act which plumbs the profoundest depths of division." [4]

The death of God therefore becomes the deepest negative moment of the self-realization of the Spirit, and all human weakness and finitude is recognized as belonging to the divine, and not outside of it. This is infinite love, redeeming all that is. But this love is, in the last analysis, the total dimension of humanity. Garaudy sums the matter up: "God is the most elevated form of self-consciousness. The final end of worship is the existence of God in man. And Hegel adds, 'That which seems to be my action is the action of God, and conversely God is only by the fact of my activity. The two beings in one, that is absolute reconciliation." [5]

The death of God has a double meaning here. One recognizes, on the one hand, remnants of the Christian drama of vicarious sacrifice for the sins of men. Indeed love, thus defined, still plays a strong role in the current Marxist philosophy of such men as Garaudy and Milan Machovec. One is tempted to say that these men believe in the love which was defined by the work of Christ, as one of the material forces moving history. On the other hand, however, the God who died for Hegel is Marx's

[4] *Dieu est Mort: Etude sur Hegel* (Paris: Presses Universitaires de France, 1962) , p. 406.

[5] *Ibid.,* pp. 127-28.

and Feuerbach's God, who was always a projection of the human imagination, the God who must be abolished in order that humanity may take his place. This is basically the theme of self-assertion, not self-denial, of conflict and victory, not of forgiveness and love. The same ambiguity expressed itself in Hegel's view of history as the dialectical process of God's self-realization in the human struggle, especially in the struggle of national cultures with one another. In his mature thought it can be seen in his logic itself. Man does not know reality in the relation of subject to object, but in the process of struggle. Reason, as distinct from mere understanding, means to grasp the inner dynamic of things in an active way. The laws of history are also the laws of knowledge itself: (1) the law of strife, interpenetration, and unity of opposites, replacing the law of contradiction, (2) the law of the transformation of quantitative into qualitative change, (3) the law of the negation of the negation. These are laws of movement, not of structure. In this movement the knower himself is involved, with his own drive toward absolute knowledge and power, or his participation in a culture that is informed with this goal. The test of true knowledge, then, is whether it prevails in the human struggle. We have in Hegel history's most intense expression of absolute humanism combined with an explanation of the forces that limit the infinity of man's possibilities—the forces of "evil"—in such a way as to show how even they contribute in the long run to his liberation.

All this was Marx's heritage. He was a Renaissance, Enlightenment, Hegelian humanist before he ever came into serious contact with the social revolution whose chief theoretician he was to become. "Free, conscious self-activity," he wrote in the Economic-Philosophical Manuscripts, "is the species character of man." But he differed from Hegel while following him, in that for him the image of suffering love was not redemptive, and the union of the self with the other was not described as love. For him the object was the occasion for struggle, for conquest. It represented an obstacle that must be organized into place. He wrote:

The practical production of an objective world, the working up of inorganic nature, is the expression of man as a conscious species being. It is in the working up of an objective world therefore that man first really proves himself as a species being. This production is his practical species life. Through it nature appears as his work, and his reality,[6]

and he sees his own reflection in that which he has made. It follows, therefore, that there must also be no interaction and mutual limitation, no I-Thou relation, between man and man. Man is a species being. As individual he is made to be universal, in harmony and solidarity with all other men in his absolute freedom. And finally there must be no absolute Other, no creator or gracious lord or redeemer, to whom one owes one's life and being. Man must be his own creator, by the power of his own work alone.

Thus Marx the humanist. But he was also, by virtue of the absoluteness of his ideal for man, history's most acute formulator of the proletarian consciousness. The

[6] *Economic and Philosophical Manuscripts,* Bottomore Translation, in Erich Fromm, *Marx's Concept of Man* (New York: Ungar, 1961), pp. 127-28.

experience of alienation was basic to his consciousness, as basic as was the movement of the Spirit to the spirit of Hegel. The processes of social existence, in his view, were dehumanizing man. The movement of material forces was directed toward the total destruction of the structures that guide these processes. The inner necessities of social development lead to contradictions that will explode the present order and create a totally new world. Man, therefore, is not called to realize his humanity in present conditions, but to accept his total dehumanization in solidarity with his fellow proletarians as an opportunity to give himself totally to the future in the revolutionary struggle. This, Marx believed, is not a moral exhortation. It is the being and the consciousness of the proletarian himself, outside of which he can only live and act in illusions. Human reason, for him, is not universal in method or content, but reflects and is the tool of man's struggle to realize himself in social existence.

In the social production of their subsistence men enter into determined and necessary relations with each other which are independent of their wills—production relations which correspond to a definite stage of development of their material productive forces. The sum of these production relations forms the economic structure of society, the real basis upon which a juridical and political superstructure arises and to which definite forms of consciousness correspond. . . . It is not the consciousness of men which determines their existence, but on the contrary it is their social existence which determines their consciousness.[7]

[7] Marx, *Introduction to the Critique of Political Economy,* Preface.

Knowledge is therefore not only relative to different points of view; it is distorted, an instrument of struggle. The claim to objective standards of truth or morals must always be hypocritical. The test of any truth is the source in the social struggle from which it comes and the practice to which it leads. "The question," wrote Marx in his second thesis on Feuerbach, "whether objective truth is an attribute of human thought is not a theoretical but a practical question. Man must prove the truth, i.e. the reality and power, the earthiness, of his thinking in practice." His famous final thesis on Feuerbach, "Philosophers have interpreted the world in various ways; the point, however, is to change it," is not just a plea for social action. It is a statement of the condition of man and his capacity for knowledge at all.

This is a revolutionary epistemology, a concept of knowledge so intimately linked to the response of the whole man to his proletarian existence in terms of the hope for a total transformation of the world that there is no basis in theory on which it can be confronted. But like every movement of human beings it has its inner history. The practice of revolution has grown apace with the powers of the modern world. The ideology of revolution, however, has shared in the crisis of every structure of meaning, including Christian ones, when experience calls its categories in question.

By what revolutionary practice must the truth of theory be proved? Marx himself only used the word "ideology" to describe the false consciousness of exploiting classes and those dependent on them, but his whole understanding of the relation between theory and practice is an implicit recognition that his own revolutionary theory and class analysis reflects the consciousness of one group in society as well. Only in the light of his faith that classes would disappear after the revolution could he claim universality proleptically for his point of view. The problem arose when events took a different turn from those Marx had predicted, in the success of the revolution.

For Lenin, unlike Marx, there was no doubt that Marxist theory itself was the absolute truth. "You cannot eliminate even one basic assumption, one substantial part of this philosophy of Marxism (it is as if it were a solid block of steel) without abandoning objective truth, without falling into the arms of bourgeois reactionary falsehood." [8] The principle of verification then became not the response of the proletariat but the success of the Communist Party in its struggle for power on behalf of the true interests of the proletariat. The doctrine then became the substance of ideological education of the masses long after the conquest of power had taken place. But then it could no longer express the social existence of an alienated proletariat. It was rather the philosophical guide of a powerful state seeking to build a new society within and to establish its ascendancy in the world. The logical consequence of this was the paradox of Stalinism, or, I believe, the contradictions that have given rise to the recent cultural revolution in China. The *spirit* of revolution must be maintained as an instrument of state power long after the basic conquest of power has taken place. The enemy, domestic as well as foreign, must therefore be exaggerated, and the "people's

[8] Marx, *Collected Works*, Vol. XIII, p. 281.

state" must be portrayed as the leader of embattled proletarians fighting conspiracies within and encirclement without. The forces that resist the state must, in a complete reversal of definitions, be called counterrevolutionary. The absolute interpreter of the laws of history, the unquestioned expresser of the consciousness of the proletariat, becomes the one-party state itself.

The self-destructiveness of this position is evident in historical events. The result has been movement in two different directions—one moderate and one radical. The moderate direction is expressed in the efforts of European Marxist philosophers to recover the original Marxist dialectic of theory and practice as a method for perceiving and acting on truth in all stages of society. "It is in the uniqueness of man's being," writes the Czech philosopher Karel Kosik, "that we can perceive the essential inner relationship between truth and man. The human reality is that point at which truth is not only revealed, but also realized." [9] Man is a being-creating entity. In the practice of his life and action he produces and renews the world which is external to him, and in this union of himself and the world, of spirit and matter, of subject and object, of product and productivity, he also understands reality. "Human practice is not practical activity as distinct from theorizing, but the determination of human being as *formation* of reality." [10] What Kosik calls the "concrete totality" is not an objective system, but rather the whole of things in process of interaction

[9] "Man and Philosophy," in *Socialist Humanism,* Erich Fromm, ed. (New York: Doubleday, 1965) , p. 170.
[10] Karel Kosik, *Dialektik des Konkreten* (Frankfort, 1967), p. 218.

with the perceiving human subject. Perception is a creative act, a part of the struggle of human self-realization, which in turn is an endless process expressed through "the totality of social relations, institutions and ideas," in which man himself is changed. This is, for Kosik, revolutionary practice, of which dialectical thought is a counterpart. He specifically rejects Herbert Marcuse's idea that the end result of Marx's transformation of Hegel's theory was a kind of scientific sociology with an operational view of truth, the precursor of modern sociology. Rather, he believes, change comes about by the dynamic interaction of theory with revolutionary action challenging structures of "pseudo-concreteness" that would arrest and distort the self-realization of man.

What has happened here is a fascinating but fundamental change in the direction of the Marxist understanding of the relation between truth and social existence. What it can mean is drawn out by the Polish philosopher Leszek Kolakowski. The value of Marxism, he says, is that it expresses in a special way the "consciousness of the limitation and distortion of social sciences under the pressure of social conditions forming the mentality of the thinker." This distortion characterizes all thought.[11] Marxism directs the mind toward seeing in each situation that part of society which is decisive in the struggle for social justice. It is a kind of living philosophical inspiration, not a universal system. It has, along with certain other schools of philosophy and the Gospels of the New Testament, the capacity to

[11] "Aktuelle und nichtaktuelle Begriffe des Marxismus," in *Der Mensch ohne Alternative* (Munich, 1960) , pp. 24 ff.

"create instruments to criticise itself over a relatively long period of time."

There is, then, in the social situation created by Marxist unity of theory and practice, as in all other situations, an inevitable tension between the orthodoxy that defends the existing system and the critical questioning that exposes its relativity and opens up the direction of change. There are always priests—and jesters.

The priest is the guardian of the absolute who upholds the cult of the final and obvious contained in the tradition. The jester is he who, although a habitué of good society, does not belong to it and makes it the object of his inquisitive impertinence—he who questions what appears to be self-evident. . . .

The jester's attitude is an endless attempt to reflect on the various arguments of contradictory ideas, an attitude dialectical by its very nature—simply to overcome what is because it is. A jester does not jeer out of sheer contrariness; he jeers because he mistrusts the stabilized world. In a world where allegedly everything has happened already, the jester's contribution is an always active imagination which thrives on the resistance it must overcome.[12]

The revolutionary has become a jester—a necessary pole in an ongoing tension. The social consciousness of alienated man struggling for total change in the structures of society has become the insight that in every society there is need to grasp the "concrete totality" of things in such a way as to transform it in the direction of greater human justice and freedom, and that every such effort is an ideological risk subject to correction in

[12] *Ibid.*, p. 276.

the give and take of society itself. This social consciousness comes very close to the best insights of liberal pragmatism, and expresses in humanistic terms some echoes
of the Hebrew-Christian understanding that man's
knowledge is continually in need of judgment and con-
version by encounter with a living God. All of this was
implicit in Marx, but it turns into a permanent methodology Marx's basic *revolutionary* impulse.

It should not be surprising, therefore, that revolutionaries in the continuing proletarian situations of this
world—in Latin America primarily—have turned elsewhere for a more radical epsitemology. Marx himself
retains his influence, but primarily because of his starting
point as viewed by the consciousness of an alienated
humanity. The Uruguayan (Christian!) philosopher
Hiber Conteris describes Latin American consciousness
as turning frankly toward the concept of ideology as the
expression of an active way of understanding and revolu-
tionizing objective reality. "When we draw attention to
the social dimension of ideology," he writes, "we are
recalling that it appears to us like a system of variable
coherence which expresses, explains or justifies the attitudes of man in relation to the world in which he lives,
and also as an incitement to act in this or that direction
in accordance with a value judgment on society." [13] Established powers, he points out, do not need ideology,
since they have force to maintain their position. They
need not reflect on the reason or justice of their position

[13] Unpublished speech at the World Conference on Church and
Society, Geneva, 1966. Conteris draws on Armand Cuvillier, *Las
Ideologias a la luz del conocimiento* (Mexico: D.F., 1967), and
Meynaud and Lancelot, *Las actitudes politicas* (Buenos Aires).

as long as it is not threatened. But for the poor, an ideological grasp on reality—an explanation and analysis of history that will show where and how the forces working for liberation and change are operating, and therefore where the hope lies—is essential to self-awareness and to human activity. This ideological approach is not necessarily a closed system; it can be—as Conteris maintains that it is in Latin America—fluid, eclectic, and pragmatic in its structures. Revolutionary experience leads to a redefinition of its rationale, according to "the need felt by the movements and groups which are ideologically creative to turn their ideas into practice, to define themselves ideologically not by reason of a purely intellectual process, but in the light of their action and their political commitment." It is the experience itself that remains constant, expressing itself in the determined search for true humanity by basic transformation of existing social structures and powers.

This revolutionary consciousness has escaped the reconciling influence of the Christian-Marxist dialogue, and indeed regards this dialogue as a part of the community of interest among economically developed classes and nations. It is a consciousness in search of an ideology that will give basis to action in which it is already engaged—action that is characterized by the negation of existing systems more than by a utopian dream of the future. But its inner crisis is defined by just this negativity and openness. In what objective, and at the same time redemptive, reality can the revolutionary *believe?* Marx had the perfect synthesis in his confidence in a social negation of the negation in the proletariat. But the modern revolutionary is too sophisticated about

89

human bias to accept it any longer. He profoundly rejects the rationality of his class or race opponents—the rationality of "development," of evolutionary, piecemeal change—but what can he place against it that is equally and objectively convincing? The trend is moving away from even attempting such an ideological confrontation. "For the training of revolutionary cadres," writes Régis Debray, "the people's war is more decisive than political activity." [14] Guerrilla warfare is, itself, the first act of self-awareness for the dispossessed. Out of experience with it will grow an understanding of the tactic of revolution, followed by a grasp of the strategy of the conquest of power and then, only at the last, an ideology. The movement, the warfare, is itself the ultimate reality. All else must flow from it. So, also, for Frantz Fanon, writing from the Algerian war, it is the act of violence against the oppressor that gives to the exploited peasant his humanity, in the light of which he can rediscover the true genius of his culture.[15] Let these examples from abroad illuminate the, as yet, chaotic situation in the urban ghettos of our own country.

It is against this background that we have to ask about the interaction of Christian and Marxist conceptions of and responses to objectivity reality. Let me conclude with three comments on this interaction.

First, the Marxist insight that human knowledge is distorted by its source in the struggle of social groups to realize their purposes in conflict with others, and is

[14] *Revolution within the Revolution?* (New York: Monthly Review Press, 1967) , p. 89.

[15] Fanon, *The Wretched of the Earth* (New York: Grove Press, 1965) .

referred to events themselves for verification, is a rediscovery of the biblical understanding of revelation and
man's response. The problem of knowledge for Christian
theology centers in the fact that revelation is never at the
disposal of human structures of thought, and that the
revealer is not "God" in any generic sense, but one who
bears the name YHWH. YHWH is a proper name. It is,
apparently, the derivative of the primitive ejaculation,
"*Ya*," which is common to many Semitic tribes and
means "he," or "this one," referring to a deity whose
name is tabu. The combined form, "*Yahweh*," means
"he who is there." In the patriarchal stories of Genesis
(the so-called Yahwist document), it designates him who
calls or is proclaimed as the lord of the historical journey.
But the key to the name—the "revelation" of it—is in
the calling and sending of Moses.

According to this story Moses, having recognized the
glory of the Lord in the burning bush and having received the promise of his power to deliver Israel from
its slavery in Egypt and guide it into a land "flowing with
milk and honey," was still not satisfied. "If I come to
the people of Israel and say to them, 'The God [*Elohim*
—the generic term] of your fathers has sent me to you,'
and they ask me, 'What is his name?' what shall I say to
them?" (Exod. 3:13) This was an ontological, or better,
an ontocratic question. Martin Buber points out that
the Hebrew form of the question, beginning with the
pronoun "what" rather than "who," indicates more than
a desire to make acquaintances. It is a question about the
substance, the nature of the god, that he may be known
in such a way as to be conjured up and to have his
power at the disposal of the people. One might translate

the question into modern terms: Given that there were certain spiritual influences that held sway over the lives of our forefathers and brought them hope and fulfillment, which if any of the *current* powers at work in the world can we make use of to do the same for us?

The Lord's answer to this question is one of the most misused texts in the Bible. The Hebrew *"ehyeh asher ehyeh"* is given several English translations, of which the most misleading is the Revised Standard Version: "I am who I am" (Exod. 3:14). *"Ehyeh"* is a transposition into the first person of *"Yahweh"* (He who is there). The future tense is supplied by the context. "I will be there as I will be there" is Buber's translation.[16] YHWH will never be captured by a human system of ideas, even the most religious. He will never fit into a structure in which his power can be used for human purposes. The question of his substance and attributes, of his "Being," is beside the point because it can only be asked according to some human concept of what Being must be. "A God," wrote Karl Barth, "about whom one can say, 'There is one,' does not exist." Who YHWH is will be known in the events of his continuing relation to the Hebrew people, the relation known in the Old Testament as the covenant. Words that describe him—including the word "God" and the word "Lord"—are forms of human response to those events in that relationship. No generic term can capture the fullness of him who establishes and maintains this relation. No human category can express it without subjecting itself to the continual

[16] Buber, *The Prophetic Faith* (New York: Harper, 1960), pp. 24 ff.

correction—the judgment and renewal—which the reality of the relation brings to its bias.

This is the negative side of the paradox of Christian knowledge. Even when he comes to us in the human form of Jesus Christ this lord is always eluding our efforts to capture him in certain formulas, always relating himself to us in new ways which demand that we recognize our old structures of values, doctrine, culture, and society as projections of our own desires, and hence idolatrous. Biblical faith is faced continually with what Gabriel Vahanian calls "the cultural self-invalidation of Christianity".[17] The people of God are constantly called into the proletarian situation by the judgment of YHWH when they are content with their own structures of faith and life, and they are called in and from that situation to respond to his promise and live by a new reality that will revolutionize the old.

But, *second,* all of this call to revolt against old structures is founded on a prior relation to reality. God; YHWH; Father, Son, and Holy Spirit, has related *himself* to man. The second of the ten commandments is based on the first—we must continually purge our graven images because he is the one before whom we shall have no other gods. It is God's initiative in reaching out for man that has intensified and deepened man's radical revolt against his world, against his religious absolutes, and ultimately against his sinful self. "It is because God himself and God alone lends our life its possibility that it becomes so impossible for us to live," wrote Karl Barth in his early revolutionary phase. "It is because the deathless

[17] *The Death of God* (New York: Braziller, 1961).

life of God is our true portion that the necessity of death reminds us so inexorably of the sinful narrowness of our will to live." [18]

We live and are given life and hope within this relation to God, beyond and despite all our distortions of this very relation itself. We are given reliable knowledge of God and of the world in relational terms even when we cannot control it with our definitions and methods. God, YHWH, the triune person, establishes a relationship and his contribution to it in ways that express our knowledge of an objective reality with which we have to do and which imposes itself on us. But *in* this relationship God reveals himself as free and sovereign. He is not bound by our descriptions and expectations. The constancy, the faithfulness, and the promise are his, not ours, and our pictures of what this relationship means are constantly being broken down and remade as we are transformed.

This means that Christians are free—indeed, called—to engage in the positive task of ideologizing about the form of our interaction with God and the world and the direction our action should take to realize the promise it contains. The report of the World Conference on Church and Society, in Geneva in 1966, says:

The discernment by Christians of what is just and unjust, human and inhuman in the complexities of political and economic change, is a discipline exercised in continual dialogue with Biblical resources, the mind of the church through history and today, and the best insights of social scientific analysis. But it remains a discipline which aims not at a

[18] "The Problem of Ethics Today," *The Word of God and the Word of Man* (New York: Harper, 1957) , p. 140.

theoretical system of truth but at action in human society. Its object is not simply to understand the world but to respond to the power of God which is recreating it. . . . Christian theology is prophetic only insofar as it dares, in full reflection, to declare how, at a particular time and place, God is at work, and thus to show the church where and when to participate in this work.[19]

This is, as the Report itself points out, to risk the formation of an ideological picture of the human situation as a guide to the church's action. It is a risk that is not only an unavoidable necessity, but one to which the Christian is called in confidence that the truth is revealed only in the relations that such committed knowledge expresses and not in some absolute system or absolute method. It is in this effort to grasp our environment with active systems of hope-filled meaning, to commit ourselves to the action they call for, and to explore their implications for the human future, that we learn to be corrected by that objective reality, the proper relation with whom we seek to express in all our acts and thoughts.

This leads to my *third* comment. To take the task of ideologizing relatively, yet seriously, commits the Christian irrevocably to a dialogue with God and with other men who grasp reality with different structures of thought. This dialogue is the vehicle of our own transformation by and in the truth.

The Geneva Report says once more,

Theology reflects not only action but interaction between God's revelation and man's ideological understanding of his

[19] *Official Report* of the World Conference on Church and Society, p. 202.

own condition and desires. Precisely insofar as the Christian is serious in seeking and acting on the command of God, believing and proclaiming it to be such, he becomes open to the correction of God out of his experience. Christians, like all human beings, are affected by ideological perspectives. But their witness is in the way in which they show themselves to be constantly corrected in their encounter with God and their neighbors while acting on their faith." [20]

This encounter engages our whole selves in the exploration of the world of relations and possibilities that our commitment has opened up. We are not masters of its consequences. It may lead to conflict with other men whose ideologies differ from ours, and this may in turn lead to the transformation of our own perspectives. It involves a process of *metanoia,* of the surrender and rediscovery of self in a new relation and a new reality, such as is possible only to those who have known what an earlier commitment means. It means that, in our firm commitment to action we believe to be God's will, we are confronted with another who lays a claim on us with his conviction, and we must understand this confrontation as an occasion for repentance and a gift of God's grace, as we struggle together to redefine our relation to the reality that includes us both and shows us our future.

It is, of course, easiest to show this process operating between Christians and Marxists who have learned to appreciate each other's insights. But this, for all its significance, is a minor test. With most of the revolutionaries of this world today, dialogue is not first of all a matter of words; it is a process of internalizing in the church itself the basic social conflict. There should be

[20] *Ibid.*

—and there are—Christian revolutionaries, as well as Christian adherents of conservative or liberal structures of society. They are acting in opposition to each other, and their words reflect a profound distrust of each other's rationality. The dialogue in this case must also be first one of acts—acts of bearing each other's hopes and fears, acts of repentance for the vast discrepancies of wealth and power that have divided us, acts of sacrifice that put the strong at the mercy of the weak, so that a new community may arise. The servanthood, the death, and the resurrection of Christ are a model of response to the world's reality which finds its deepest meaning where conflicts go beyond the realm of words.

Christian Theology
in a World in Revolution

PAUL LEHMANN

During the third week of September, 1967, the third and final preparatory Consultation for the Third Assembly of the Christian Peace Conference, scheduled for early April, 1968 in Prague, met in Bucharest, Rumania. The work of the Consultation was carried on mainly by five groups dealing with theological problems, international problems, economic questions, the "Third world," the "Peace Service of Youth," and the theme of the Prague Assembly, which was "Seek Peace and Pursue It." As a member of the group dealing with theological problems, I noted with particular attention an epigrammatic remark made at one of our sessions by the Chairman of the Consultation, Joseph Hromadka. We were discussing

the relation between Christian theology and the phenomenon of revolution. At the Prague Assembly in 1964,
the Youth Commission had declared in its report: "What
we need most of all is a theology of revolution. But
perhaps first of all we need a revolution in theology."
Very probably with this declaration in mind, Dr.
Hromadka brought into sharp focus the question of theology in a world in revolution. "I have no theology *of*
revolution," he said. "But I do have a theology *for*
revolution!"

This remark has lingered with me as a word of caution
and as a word of light. Let me suggest three considerations that may clarify our grasp of the theme and add a
modicum of precision to the discussion of it. The first
consideration may be identified by the phrase, "revolutionary theology and a theology of revolution"; the
second, by the phrase, "the Marxist-Leninist occasion";
and the third, by the phrase, "messianism, humanization,
and the problem of power."

Revolutionary Theology and Theology of Revolution

The phrase, "a theology of revolution," is a convenient
way of saying the wrong thing. As with many wrong
formulations, the error is not total. The phrase does
express a grain of truth, perhaps two grains. It does
connect two fundamental factors of human life in this
mid-twentieth-century world, and it makes this connection with a kind of insistent intimacy of which the pos-
sessive preposition is a forceful sign. "A theology *of*
revolution" denotes a confrontation between a formative
way of looking at life and of living it *and* a formative way

99

of living life and of looking at it. When Marx set up his eleventh thesis on Feuerbach, he might have had theology also in mind. "Philosophers have done nothing more than interpret the world in various ways," he wrote, "our business is to change it."[1] Theology has often joined philosophy in detaching a way of looking at life from the living of life. In Hegel, the dynamics of the self-containment of thought exhibited itself with such comprehensive and contagious power as not only to have enveloped Christian theology but, more decisively, to have inverted the ancient Socratic bond between ideas and institutions.[2] According to the Socratic traditions, ideas are the critical weapons of institutions; for Hegel, institutions are the critical weapons of ideas. Small wonder that Marx made an important note of the fact that "the weapon of criticism cannot replace the criticism of weapons."[3]

[1] Karl Marx, *Theses on Feuerbach*, No. 11; quoted by Otto Ruele, *Karl Marx* (New York: Viking Press, 1935), p. 92.

[2] This is a moot point in Hegelian scholarship. An increasingly lively discussion is going on over the question of the absoluteness and the comprehensiveness of Hegel's idealism. This discussion is tending toward a revision of a long held notion that Hegel's idealism led straight to the Prussian imperial state and consequently to a deprecation of democracy. See, for example, among others, Claude Bruaire, *L'Affirmation de Dieu, Logique et religion cretienne dans la philosophie de Hegel* (Paris: Seuil, 1965); Paul Ricoeur, De l'interpretation, *Essai sur Freud* (Seuil, 1965), esp. Book I; also Ricoeur, *Histoire de Verite* (Seuil, 1955); also Richard Kroner, *Between Faith and Thought* (New York: Oxford University Press, 1966), esp. chap. XIII. However, this discussion scarcely alters the fact that Marx and his contemporaries, both for and against Hegel, understood Hegel in such a way as to take up positions for and against Marx's criticism.

[3] Marx, *Zur Kritik der Hegelschen Rechtsphilosophie* (Introduction to the Criticism of Hegel's Philosophy of Right), 1844.

We may leave open the question whether Marx's omission of specific mention of theologians among those who "explain the world" is to be regarded as a "Freudian slip" on Marx's part or on God's. The omission happens to correspond with another though minor, part of the theological record. Christian theology has always been focally concerned with the basics of life in this world and at the same time has been uneasy about its explanation and implementation of this concern. Social involvement and social criticism have been and are intrinsic to the doing of theology in a Christian context. The roots of this connection and tension between involvement and criticism lie deep in Israel's prophetic tradition and in Jesus' personal exemplification in word and deed of his prophetic heritage. In the "koine" of the moment, Jesus put his mouth and his life "where the action is." To speak of a theology *of* revolution is, thus, rather misleading than wrong. It goes wrong when its "mis-leads" begin to be programmed. The "mis-leads" of the phrase, "theology of revolution," may be identified by two familiar theological words—"apostasy" and "idolatry." Applied to a revolutionary historical situation or movement, apostasy is the transposition of theological conceptions, otherwise derived and intended, into the semantics of social upheaval and transformation. In J. M. Lochman's account of it, it is the danger that . . . we shall be overcome by a spell of "theological giddiness." By this I mean that we shall lose theological independence, that the gospel will simply become adapted to the new situation and ideology. . . . Consider the extent to

---

See *Works, Marx-Engels,* Collected Edition, Part I, Vol. I (Frankfort, 1927) , p. 614.

which Christianity in the feudal age became feudalized
—even to the most subtle problems of theology! And in
the bourgeois epoch Christianity became simply
—bourgeois! Why, then, in a socialist epoch should a
"socialist Christianity" not come into being? [4] Idolatry,
on the other hand, is the appropriation of the sanctions
implied in theological conceptions for the purpose of
justifying a given revolutionary rationale or movement.
One thinks, for example, of the strong words of the
Barmen Declaration, reaffirming the First Command-
ment against the rising tide of acceptance by the churches
in Germany of the National Socialist movement and its
government. The pathos and subtlety of the temptation
to idolatry are movingly recalled in Eberhard Bethge's
magnificent biography of Dietrich Bonhoeffer. We are
asked to ponder a scene, not to rush to a value judgment.
On March 21, 1933, in the Garrison Church in Potsdam,
Adolf Hitler cleverly took captive the imagination of the
German people. Previous to this gathering, while Hitler
and his propaganda minister, Goebbels, held their "de-
votions" at the graves of party heroes, the President of
the Republic, von Hindenburg, together with Protestant
deputies of the Reichstag, attended a service at the Nico-
laikirche. Bishop Otto Dibelius was the preacher. In the
course of his sermon, Dibelius found it possible to
declare: "The office of Government dare not mistake
itself for personal caprice. Where order is truly established, righteousness and love must prevail!" The story

[4] Lochman, "The Service of the Church in a Socialist Society," in
The Church Amid Revolution, Harvey Cox, ed. (New York:
Association Press, 1967), p. 50.

goes that a few days before this sermon, Bonhoeffer had been invited to tea with Dibelius. In the course of the conversation, Bonhoeffer declared that the time had come for the church to desist from acclamations.[5] Although Dibelius had included passages of generous acclamation in the same sermon, he had foreshadowed, by way of a small but courageous hint, the struggle against revolutionary idolatry which he was destined to wage with increasing, if not unblemished, fortitude until his death in 1967. The struggle involved him in the eastern as well as in the western forms of the revolutionary dynamism of the world in which we still live. No model revolutionary himself, Dibelius was certainly no Reichsbischof Mueller. The doings in the Garrison Church and in the Nicolai Church thrust him into the position of Hitler's opposite number. This juxtaposition is a sign of the peril of idolatry to which a theology of revolution is exposed.

It has often been noted that there is a world of difference between the National Socialist and the Marxist-Leninist revolutions in our time. The theological force of this difference, however, has not always been clearly discerned or adequately underlined. One could say that Marxism-Leninism, at the theoretical level, has been sensitive to the perils both of apostasy and of idolatry, whereas National Socialism was sensitive to neither, committing both with impunity. More generally stated, this is the fundamental theological importance of the distinction between revolution and counterrevolution. A

[5] Eberhard Bethge, *Dietrich Bonhoeffer* (Munich: Chr. Kaiser, 1967) , p. 315.

genuinely revolutionary movement is not immune to the perils of apostasy and idolatry, but is sensitive to both. Counterrevolution is both insensitive and vulnerable to these perils. If, for example, we make a slight alteration in the phrase, "a theology *of* revolution," and speak instead of "a theory *for* revolution," we may find this point instructively exhibited by two passages from Lenin's *State and Revolution*.

At the outset of the essay, Lenin remarks:

What is now happening to Marx's teaching has, in the course of history, happened repeatedly to the teachings of revolutionary thinkers and leaders of oppressed classes struggling for emancipation. During the lifetime of great revolutionaries, the oppressing classes constantly hounded them, received their teachings with the most savage malice, the most furious hatred and the most reckless campaigns of lies and slander. After their death, attempts are made to convert them into harmless icons, to canonize them, so to say, and to surround their *names* with a certain halo for the "consolation" of the oppressed classes and for the purpose of duping them, while at the same time emasculating the *content* of the revolutionary teaching, blunting its revolutionary edge and vulgarizing it.[6]

This, I venture to suggest, is a succinct formulation of the secular meaning of apostasy. The humanizing thrust of revolutionary sensitivity and insight is diverted from its transforming purpose by semantic legerdemain. The success of apostasy is proportional to the wizardry of its word games.

[6] Vladimir Lenin, *The State and Revolution* in *Essential Works of Marxism*, with an introduction and commentaries by Arthur P. Mendel (New York: Bantam Books, 1961), p. 103. Lenin's classic first appeared in 1919.

Toward the end of the essay, in the course of a scathing attack upon Kautsky as an opportunist, and upon anarchists, at the opposite end of the revolutionary spectrum, Lenin declares, with reference to the example of the Commune:

Marx's critic-analytical genius perceived in the practical measures of the Commune the *turning point,* which the opportunists fear and do not want to recognize because of their cowardice, because they do not want to break irrevocably with the bourgeoisie, and which the anarchists do not want to perceive, either because they are in a hurry or because they do not understand at all the conditions of great social changes. "We must not even think of destroying the old state machine; how can we get along without ministries and officials?" argues the opportunist, who is completely saturated with philistinism, and who, at bottom, not only does not believe in revolution, in the creative power of revolution, but lives in mortal dread of it. . . . "We must think *only* of destroying the old state machine; it is no use probing into the *concrete* lessons of earlier proletarian revolutions and analyzing *what* to put in the place of what has been destroyed, and *how*"—argues the anarchist. . . . Consequently, the tactics of the anarchist become the tactics of *despair* instead of a ruthlessly bold revolutionary effort to solve concrete problems while taking into account the practical conditions of the mass movement.[7]

This, I venture to suggest, is a succinct formulation of the secular meaning of idolatry. The humanizing thrust of revolutionary sensitivity and insight is deprived of its transforming purpose by the self-justifying satisfaction of simplistic immediacy. The business of idols is to dispense approval "on the spot."

Whether understood and practiced as theological or

[7] *Ibid.,* pp. 195-96. Italics are Lenin's.

as secular errors, these twin dogmatisms imperil the dynamics and the *human* meaning and purpose of social change. In doing so, they call sharply into question the adequacy either of a *theology* of revolution or of a *theory* of revolution for understanding "at all the conditions of great social changes." Indeed, these dogmatisms "zero in" upon Lenin's momentous transformation of Marx's epochal discovery of the functional relation between ideas and social reality. As Marx reports his insight and analyzes it, the relation between ideas and social reality is one of power: the power of ideas; the power of social reality in movement, transition, and transformation; the power of social reality to shape ideas and, in turn, of ideas to shape social reality. The critical instance of the connection between ideas and power is force, or—as, wittingly or unwittingly, we are learning again to join Marx in identifying—violence. Thus, as the *German Ideology* puts it: "Not criticism, but revolution, is the motive force of history." [8] And Lenin quotes Engels' use of Marx's famous metaphor in making the point that force plays another role in history than that of diabolical power, namely, a revolutionary role. "In the words of Marx," says Engels, "it [revolutionary force] is the midwife of every old society which is pregnant with a new one; it is the instrument with the aid of which social movement forces its way through and shatters the dead, fossilized political forms." [9] When Marx underlined the

[8] Marx, *Die Deutsche Ideologie* (Berlin: Dietz, 1957), p. 35. Translation mine. The treatise was first published in co-authorship with Engels in 1845-46.

[9] *The State and Revolution* in *Essential Works of Marxism,* p. 115. Lenin quotes from Engels' *Anti-Duehring,* 3rd German edition, part II, end of chap. IV. Brackets mine.

operational link between the power of ideas and ideas of power, either for resisting or for effecting social change, he discovered and called it ideology. It remained, then, for Lenin to transform the Marxian analysis of the power of ideology into an ideology of power.[10]

We shall return to the question of ideology. Meanwhile, we must consider the possibility that the phenomenon of ideology requires us on theological as well as on sociopolitical grounds to explore an alternative both to a theology and to a theory *of* revolution. It is this possibility that gives pertinence to the distinction between a theology *of* revolution and a theology *for* revolution. It gives pertinence also to the scandalizing implication that a theology *for* revolution can deal *more* constructively with the dynamics of radical social change and the perils attending it than a theory *of* revolution can. The mere suggestion of such a "more" is almost certain to evoke a fury of debate, dissent, and even ridicule. In the light of the antirevolutionary stance of the theological tradition and of the antitheological stance of Marxism-Leninism, such a "more" can scarcely be more than sheer ideological intransigence, beyond the pale of serious attention. On the other hand, to attempt a case for such a "more" on the basis of a possibility rather than of the record is to court the rejection reserved for all ad hominem reasoning. At the level of serious interpretation, such reasoning is immoral. It is cheating. Perhaps the most scandalizing implication of such a "more" is its refusal to allow to revolutionary

[10] I have noted this development and elaborated somewhat upon it in an earlier essay, viz., *Ideology and Incarnation* (Geneva: The John Knox Association, 1962) , pp. 18-23.

theory the corrections of historical experience, the bene-
fit of hindsight, as it were, readily granted to theological
analysis.

Nevertheless, theological analysis cannot avoid the of-
fense (σκάνδαλον) of such a scandalizing "more." Christian theology, at any rate, cannot avoid it. Intrinsic
to Christian theology is a dynamic conceptual response
to a moving experience of a historical presence whose
renewing power begins with the freedom of a binding
commitment and functions with enlarging inclusiveness
as *the* power of renewal of man in himself and of "man
in his communities." [11] The bearer of this presence identifies in his person the beginning and the end; the source
and fulfillment of order and meaning, of nature and
history, of man and society. His name is Jesus, Messiah
—in Pascal's words, "the end of all things and the center
to which all tends." [12] Or, as the letter to the Colossians
puts it:

He is the image of the invisible God, the first-born of all
creation; for in him all things were created, in heaven and on
earth, visible and invisible, whether thrones or dominions or
principalities or authorities—all things were created through
him and for him. He is before all things, and in him all
things hold together. For in him all the fullness of God was
pleased to dwell, and through him to reconcile to himself all
things, whether on earth or in heaven, making peace by the
blood of his cross.[13]

In and by his presence, science and philosophy, culture

[11] Reinhold Niebuhr, *Man in His Communities* (New York:
Scribner's, 1965).
[12] Blaise Pascal, *Pensees* (New York: Dutton, 1931), Fr. 555.
[13] Col. 1:15-17, 19, 20 RSV.

and politics, acquire a humanizing occasion, context, and point. They know what they are for and are pursued for the sake of what they know. The outward signs of his presence in, with, and under this knowledge and pursuit are reverence, righteousness, and reconciliation. The fruits of his presence are joy and peace in the Holy Spirit, on earth among men—all men—in the favor of God.

The renewing power of this Presence to release its power of renewal has been focally and forcefully described by W. H. Auden in a Christmas Oratorio, which he calls *For the Time Being.* At once faithful to Colossians and actual in our world in revolution, Mr. Auden's reflections upon the *Nativity* seem to say exactly where we are and what a theology for revolution is really all about.

By the event of this birth the true significance of all other events is defined, for of every other occasion it can be said that it could have been different, but of this birth it is the case that it could in no way be other than it is. And by the existence of this Child, the proper value of all other existences is given, for of every other creature it can be said that it has extrinsic importance but of this Child it is the case that He is in no sense a symbol.

We have right to believe that we really exist.

By Him is dispelled the darkness wherein the fallen will cannot distinguish between temptation and sin, for in Him we become fully conscious of Necessity as our freedom to be tempted, and of Freedom as our necessity to have faith. And by Him is illuminated the time in which we execute those choices through which our freedom is realised or prevented, for the course of History is predictable in the degree to which all men love themselves, and spontaneous in the degree to which each man loves God and through Him his neighbour.

109

The distresses of choice are our chance to be blessed.

Because in Him all passions find a logical In-Order-That,
by Him is the perpetual recurrence of Art assured.

Safe in His silence, our songs are at play.

Because in Him abstraction finds a
passionate For-The-Sake-Of,
by Him is the continuous development of Science assured.

Our lost Appearances are saved by His love.

For the Truth is indeed One, without which is no salvation,
but the possibilities of real knowledge are as many as are the
creatures in the very real and most exciting universe that God
creates with and for His love, and it is not Nature which is
one public illusion, but we who have each our private illusions
about Nature.

Its errors forgiven, may our Vision come home.[14]

Thus, Christian theology is rooted in celebration and
seeks to give a conceptual description of it. The celebration concerns a messianic presence and power in a world
in revolution. The lines from Colossians, as well as those
from the Christmas Oratorio, seem, to this reader, to
identify the point at which and from which the referent,
the context, the process, and the power of humanization
converge. A theology for revolution is an analytical
undertaking that tries, by conceptual means, to explore
the bearing of the relation between messianism and hu-

[14] W. H. Auden, "For the Time Being," in *Collected Poetry*
(New York: Random House, 1945), pp. 451-54. Mr. Auden's order
has been adapted, esp. the interspersed five lines, which in the
original are a refrain by the Chorus, in response to "The Medita-
tion of Simeon." Hopefully, the present adaptation may help to
intensify the transforming actuality of the dialectical relation between the Vision of the Nativity and the human response to it.

manization upon the fact and the dynamics of revolutionary social change. The celebration, together with the conceptual aim and effort of a theology *for* revolution, comprises a genuinely revolutionary theology. In such a theology, sensitivity to the perils of apostasy and idolatry grows in proportion to sensitivity to the fundamental, yet always contemporary, self-critical and socio-critical relation between messianism and humanization. Having identified the focus and framework of a theology for revolution, it remains for us also to identify the focus and framework of revolution. Then we should be able to spy out the land of promise in order to be accounted worthy to enter into it. Let us hope that we may come out as Caleb and Joshua did, and not be numbered among those ten who "know how to interpret the appearance of earth and sky; but . . . do . . . not know how to interpret the present time"—their time in theirs, our time in ours.[15]

The Marxist-Leninist Occasion

The revolution in theology called for by the Youth Commission at Prague in 1964 properly begins not with a theology *of* revolution, but with a theology *for* revolution. But can we also identify the focus and framework of revolution for which such a theology is to be explored? Here again, Lenin may help us to see what we are about. He writes:

What is at issue is neither opposition nor political struggle in general, but *revolution*. Revolution consists in the proletariat

[15] Luke 12:56 (RSV) ; see Num. 14 and 15.

destroying the "administrative apparatus" and the *entire* state machine, replacing it with a new one, consisting of the armed workers. . . . The point is whether the old state machine (bound by thousands of threads to the bourgeoisie and permeated through and through with routine and inertia) shall remain, or be *destroyed* and replaced by a *new* one. Revolution consists not in the new class commanding, governing with the aid of the *old* state machine, but in the class *smashing* this machine and commanding, governing with the aid of a *new* machine. Kautsky slurs over this *basic* idea of Marxism or completely fails to understand it.[16]

"Revolution consists not in the new class commanding, governing with the aid of the old state machine, but in the class smashing this machine and commanding, governing with the aid of a new machine." This is the revolution to which a revolutionary theology must respond!

In retrospect, it is easy to disregard Lenin's formulation of our problem as having been overtaken by events. We have been telling ourselves for almost a quarter of a century now that among the foremost errors of Marxism-Leninism is its rigid insistence that capitalist nation-states were foredoomed by the dynamics of internal decay to succumb to the contradiction between fruitless internecine rivalries, on the one hand, and paralyzing civil conflict on the other. Instead, the so-called bourgeois political economy has manifested suprising powers of adaptation to the stresses and strains of war, of domestic and foreign competition; and the rhythm which embodies the relations between rising national productivity

[16] Lenin *The State and Revolution* in *Essential Works of Marxism*, pp. 193-94. Italics are Lenin's.

112

and recessions proceeds along a kind of upward spiral, on which the recessions get less severe and the gross national income steadily mounts. Consequently, the working class acquires as well as produces goods and services; and what has "withered away" is not the state but the proletarian character of the working class itself. There simply is no new class available to smash the old state machine.

Furthermore, there is the awkward geopolitical circumstance that the great Marxist-Leninist experiment has taken root and flourished in a previously agrarian, peasant, and industrially underdeveloped country, not in an advanced industrial and technological society. The line between East and West is drawn, therefore, not between advanced Western capitalist societies, undergoing inevitable proletarianization, and backward Eastern agrarian societies, awaiting revolutionary liberation and transformation. The line between East and West is a boundary marked by a fragile river and spheres of influence. The river brings the East farther west than ever before, and deprives the West of effective buffer protection. The spheres of influence signal the power struggle between two giant technological, industrial complexes for world hegemony, if not domination. At once drawn toward each other, these two complexes manage to prolong a precarious peace by a balance of power which nuclear and orbital competition has gradually transformed into a "balance of terror."

Meanwhile, the objectives of this East-West rivalry are exhibiting a dynamics of their own. It is the dynamics of underdevelopment that is beginning to take shape in the so-called Third World. In their own way drawn

113

together by long overdue socioeconomic transformations and pulled apart by tribal and nationalistic traditions and rivalries, the peoples and governments of these changing and emerging nation-states conduct foreign policies designed to exploit the hostilities of the Cold War to optimum advantage, and pursue domestic policies designed to exacerbate the relations between the peoples and their governments by preventing the radical transformation of the bases of power. One example may suffice, and it is fitting that it should come to us from that portion of the Third World nearest to us as North Americans. Writing in the *Christian Century* about "The New Latin Revolutionaries and the U.S.," Richard Shaull tells us that

For a brief period in the early 1960s the success of efforts to awaken and organize the masses, together with the opening up of opportunities for a new leadership, made it possible for many to hope that this sort of national development could be achieved by means of the democratic process. Then came the military coup in Brazil, U.S. intervention in the Dominican Republic, the systematic exclusion of the younger progressive leadership from positions of influence, the gradual disillusionment with Christian democracy in Chile. Today it is all too clear that the traditional leadership groups in Latin America, though unable to bring about either economic development or a new social order, are going to do everything possible to preserve their position of power.

Only two roads are open for the new generation. The most appealing is that of guerrilla movements of national liberation, of which the late Che Guevara and the late Fr. Camilo Torres are the outstanding symbols. . . .

A few revolutionaries, perhaps a growing number, are searching for an alternative strategy—one which might best be described as a long-term struggle to create the political equivalent of guerrilla warfare, along with a program for systematic "subversion" of institutions. . . .

Whatever the ideological background or present strategy of the new revolutionaries, they all regard the United States as The Enemy.[17]

One would like to be able to conclude that the combination of Marxist-Leninist errors in sociopolitical analysis with the dynamics of underdevelopment and technological overdevelopment, signalized by the emergence of the Third World, has moved us effectively beyond Lenin's identification of the revolution to which a theology for revolution must respond. But can we really run such a risk without ending up in the ostrich corner? Indeed, have we not really been steadily driven into that corner by the too welcome supposition that the analytical errors of Marxism-Leninism have invalidated its insights into the meaning and focus of revolution? And if we have managed to escape falling into this temptation, have we not fallen prey to the alternate one? This is to mistake the revolutionary experimentation of a world in revolution as a sign of the complexity and flexibility of social change that render the Marxist-Leninist understanding of revolution obsolete. Do these twin temptations not really "hang us up"—those of us who are neither orthodox nor party Marxists, and who try somehow to find our periscopic way with the aid of a theological lens—on the dilemma between the contentment at having moved beyond Marxism and the confusion that arises from the conviction that since we do not know

[17] *The Christian Century*, Vol. LXXXV, No. 3 (Jan. 17, 1968), pp. 69-70.

exactly where we are going, we had better go on exactly as we are? These questions sound rhetorical. Actually they come to mind as a way of facing the pervasive subtlety of the anticommunist stance in a world in revolution. It is a subtlety worthy of Secretary of State Dean Rusk, if he were but worthy of the subtlety.

Plainly, there is more than one assessment of the phenomenon of revolution, just as there is more than one theological response to it. It has, however, become ever clearer to us in the course of these reflections that we might well pause over a possibly wrong turn in the road before we set out in search of possibly right turns. Such a pause begins by our recognizing that while we are living in a post-Christian world, we are not living in a post-Marxian one. Marxism-Leninism is still the bearer of the revolutionary ferment of our time. It is the bearer of this ferment in the sense that despite the stresses and strains of power, of heresy and schism within the communist movement, the Marxist-Leninist account of the impact of power upon social change and of social change upon power is still the point from which to take our bearings in the revolutionary situation in which we live.

In two definitive respects, Lenin clarified the Marxian account of the midwifery of revolution as a historical force. The first underlines the relation between revolution and the state; the second underlines the relation between revolution and humanization. I shall reserve attention to the second clarification for the succeeding section and try to understand what the first clarification involves.

As regards the state, I am suggesting that Lenin's almost epigrammatic remark, already mentioned, has not been overtaken by events. "Revolution consists not in the new class commanding, governing with the aid of the old state machine, but in the class smashing this machine and commanding, governing with the aid of a new machine." The state *is* the machinery of government, and government is the control center of the state. Taken together, state and government are the foci of effective power in human society. Whatever may be the case with primordial human communities, which seem so akin to animal "communities," bound together by natural forces of cohesion and authority, the development of reason and power seems to mark the widening distance between man and his animal and social past. Reason and power thus become the chief characteristics of community as human. "A social instinct," said Aristotle, "is implanted in all men by nature, and yet he who first founded the state was the greatest of all benefactors." Earlier by nearly a century—and it may be also by profundity—Thucydides had observed: "Of the gods we believe, and of men we know, that by a necessary law of their nature they rule wherever they can." [18] Obviously, the forms of government vary, as do also the operational styles of control of the state machinery. But there can be no effective

[18] Quoted by Reinhold Niebuhr, *Man in His Communities,* pp. 35-36. The passage from Aristotle is *Politics,* Bk. I, chap. ii, sec. 15; from Thucydides, *History of the Peloponnesian War,* Bk. 5, chap. 105. Niebuhr sees in these two observations a clue to the roots of realistic and idealistic motifs in Western political theory. The "idealistic" confidence in reason hoped, by the time of the Renaissance and Enlightenment, for the displacement of strong governments of power elites by ever more harmonious communities. The "realistic" understanding of power "was not analyzed until the nineteenth century, when both Freud and Marx elaborated their theories of rationalization and ideology." Cf. *Ibid.,* p. 37.

117

social change apart from a change at the control center of power; and conversely, the dynamics of social change are such that when reason and power fail to create justice in freedom for men in society, reason and power give way to *force majeure*.

It is not accidental that Western political theory has, since its beginning, identified justice as the foundation of civil society (i.e., of human community) and thus as the criterion of the right relation between reason and power. At the operational level, justice, in the context of what Reinhold Niebuhr has called "idealistic theories of community," came to be practiced according to the maxim of the *suum cuique*. In the context of "realistic theories of community" (Niebuhr), justice came to be practiced according to the maxim: "From each according to his ability; to each according to his need." But in either case, the achievement of justice has been the fragile fruit of a precarious success of reason over power, and, more often than not, the bitter victim of the triumph of power over freedom. Long before Lenin, Cato had declared that:

Even from the very beginning of the state wrongs were committed by the more powerful, which led to the separation of the people from the fathers, and besides which there were other internal dissensions; and the only time at which there existed a just and moderate administration was after the banishment of the kings, and *that* no longer than whilst they had cause to be afraid of Tarquin, and were carrying on the grievous war which had been undertaken on his account against Etruria; but afterwards the fathers oppressed the people as slaves, flogged them as the kings had done, drove them from their land, and, to the exclusion of all others, held the government in their own hands alone. And to these discords, whilst the fathers were wishing to rule, and the people were unwilling to serve, the second Punic war put an end; for again great fear began to press upon their disquieted minds, holding them back from those distractions by another and greater anxiety, and bringing them back to civil concord.[19]

Long after Cato, and within fifty years of the initial publication of Lenin's classic on *The State and Revolution,* Engels had noted, in his Preface to Marx's analysis of *The Civil War in France* (1871),

According to the philosophical conception, the state is "the realization of the idea", or the Kingdom of God on earth, translated into philosophical terms, the sphere in which eternal truth and justice is or should be realized. And from this follows a superstitious reverence for the state and everything connected with it. . . . People think that they have taken quite an extraordinarily bold step forward when they have rid themselves of belief in hereditary monarchy and swear by the democratic republic. In reality, however, the state is nothing but a machine for the oppression of one class by another, in the democratic republic no less than in the monarchy. At best the state is an evil inherited by the proletariat after its victorious struggle for class supremacy, . . . until such time as a generation reared in new, free social conditions is able to throw the entire lumber of the state on the scrap heap.[20]

Engels, of course, had Hegel and Bismarck's Germany in mind. But the dynamics of social change, at an accelerating tempo, enlarged the scope and confirmed the focus of Engels' analysis. Marx and Engels had glimpsed

[19] Augustine, *The City of God,* trans. by Marcus Dods (New York: Modern Library), Bk. V, ch. 12, p. 162. Italics mine.

[20] Quoted by Lenin in *The State and Revolution,* pp. 163-64.

possibilities across the Channel, on account of which they had excluded England from their sociopolitical conclusions about the Continent. There, a minimal bureaucracy and the absence of a militarist clique seemed to make for the possibility even of a people's revolution. But by 1917, Lenin could write that:

> Today, . . . this restriction made by Marx is no longer valid. Both England and America, the biggest and the last representatives—in the whole world—of Anglo-Saxon "liberty", in the sense that they had no militarist cliques and bureaucracy, have completely sunk into the . . . bloody morass of bureaucratic-military institutions which subordinate everything to themselves, trample everything under foot. Today, both in England and in America, "the preliminary condition for every real people's revolution" is the *smashing,* the *destruction* of the "ready-made state machinery" brought in those countries to "European", general imperialist, perfection in the years 1914-17.[21]

When a former President of the United States, and Marx, Engels, and Lenin worry, in almost the same language, about power, government, and social change, it would be irresponsibly naïve to conclude with the founder of the John Birch Society that General Eisenhower has obviously become a "fellow-traveller." A nation and its policy-makers are better advised to face the coincidence as a sobering sign of an ominous shadow over the shape of things to come. Among his valedictory *obiter dicta,* President Eisenhower wondered aloud about the human future of American society, involved, as he saw it, in a dynamics of development under the aegis of

[21] Lenin, *Ibid.,* p. 130. Italics are Lenin's.

what he called "the industrial-military complex." Almost
a century earlier, Marx had firmly declared "that the
next attempt of the French Revolution will be no longer,
as before, to transfer the bureaucratic-military machine
from one hand to another, but to *smash* it, and this is
the preliminary condition for every real people's revolution on the Continent." [22] Lenin then picked up this
declaration, and wrote, "The words 'to smash the bureaucratic-military machine' briefly express the principal
lesson of Marxism regarding the task of the proletariat in
relation to the state." [23] Between Marx and Lenin, on
the one hand, and between Lenin and Eisenhower, on
the other (at almost half-century intervals) the "ready-
made state machinery" has been brought, not only in
England and America, but in Lenin's own revolutionary
society, the Soviet Union, "to 'European' general im-
peralist perfection," not only "in the years 1914-17" but
in the years 1939-45 and their aftermath, and to unantici-
pated, though internally necessary technological perfection. As Herbert Marcuse has put it, with not a little
foreboding:

Technical progress, extended to a whole system of domination and coordination, creates forms of life (and of power)
which appear to reconcile the forces opposing the system and
to defeat or refute all protest in the name of historical pros-
pects of freedom from toil and domination. Contemporary
society seems to be capable of containing social change—
qualitative change which would establish essentially different

[22] In a letter to Kugelmann, on April 12, 1871, at the time of the
Paris Commune. The italics are Marx's, and his word was
zerbrechen.
[23] Lenin, *The State and Revolution*, p. 129.

institutions, a new direction of the productive process, new modes of human existence. . . . In this society, the productive apparatus tends to become totalitarian to the extent to which it determines not only the socially needed occupations, skills, and attitudes, but also individual needs and aspirations. . . . As a technological universe, advanced industrial society is a *political* universe, the latest stage in the realization of a specific historical *project*—namely, the experience, transformation, and organization of nature as the mere stuff of domination. . . . Technological rationality has become political rationality.[24]

Thus, the story of the state, from Cato to Engels, Marx, and Lenin, and on to Herbert Marcuse, is the story of "the state and revolution." Power separates "the people from the fathers" as disruptively as it separates kings from their subjects; and, in modern times, it separates the power elites from the "socially needed occupations, skills, and attitudes" and from "individual needs and aspirations." In their turn, the people are oppressed and enslaved, disquieted by fear and powerlessness, and, in the long course of human events, deprived by the technical containment of social change of "new modes of human existence." We could agree, indeed, with the pirate who, according to Augustine, had been seized by Alexander the Great. "When that king had asked the

---

[24] *One-dimensional Man* (Boston: Beacon Press, 1964; paperback, 5th printing, 1968), pp. xiv-xvi. Italics are the author's. Marcuse explains that the term "project" emphasizes the element of freedom and responsibility in historical determination. "It links autonomy and contingency"; it is also used in this way by Sartre. One may wonder, however, whether the term is not itself a technologically oriented one. Why speak of "project," for example, rather than of an "historical achievement" or "creation" or "achievement" or even "form" (*Gestalt,* in Troeltsch's sense)?

man what he meant by keeping hostile possession of the sea, he answered with bold pride, 'What thou meanest by seizing the whole earth; but because I do it with a petty ship, I am called a robber, whilst thou who dost it with a great fleet art styled an emperor.' " The pirate seemed to Augustine also to have answered affirmatively his own searching question: "Justice being taken away, then, what are kingdoms but great robberies?" [25] In short, "the earthly city, . . . though it be mistress of the nations, is itself ruled by its lust of rule." [26]

The insistent combination of the power to rule with the absence of justice makes violence inevitable. Violence is the sign of the application of the revolutionary *force majeure* to the power of the state. It points to an emerging impasse between the dynamics of social development and the existing organization of social and administrative power operative through the machinery of the state. Marxist language is sharp and unequivocal. The key words are "smash" and "destroy." Less clear is the manner of the violence. Lenin, however, does not seem to envisage indiscriminate destruction. This is why he insists so strongly upon the connection in Marx's thought of the idea of the dictatorship of the proletariat with the idea of the class struggle. He declares:

The teaching of the class struggle, when applied by Marx to the question of the state and of the socialist revolution, leads

[25] Augustine, *City of God,* Bk. IV, chap. 4. Cicero had recorded the anecdote in *De. Repub.* iii.

[26] Augustine, *Ibid.,* Bk. I, chap. 1. The original is so beautiful in its moving conciseness that it may be given here: *Unde etiam de terrena civitate, . . . etsi populi serviant, ipsa ei dominandi libido dominatur.*

of necessity to the recognition of the *political rule* of the proletariat, of its dictatorship, i.e., of power shared with none and relying upon the armed force of the masses. The overthrow of the bourgeoisie can be achieved only by the proletariat becoming transformed into the *ruling class,* capable of crushing the inevitable and desperate resistance of the bourgeoisie, and organizing *all* the laboring and exploited masses for the new economic order.[27]

The lessons that Marx and Engels had drawn from the Paris Commune were underscored by Lenin as pointing toward both the inevitability and the limits of violence. Although this "second French Revolution" was short-lived, it did discover both "the form . . . under which the economic emancipation of labor can take place" and against *what* the armed power of the workers was to be directed, i.e., against the "centralized government, army, political police, bureaucracy." [28] The Commune, however, failed to press the advantages of these discoveries with sufficient determination. Destined, as Marx had said, "not only to supersede the monarchical form of class-rule, but class-rule itself," [29] it could not enter into its historical fulfillment. This remained for a time when "the organ of suppression" should become

the majority of the population, and not a minority, as was always the case under slavery, serfdom and wage slavery. And since the majority of the people *itself* suppresses its oppressors, a "special force" for suppression is *no longer necessary!* In this sense the state *begins to wither away.* Instead of the special institutions of a privileged minority

[27] *The State and Revolution,* p. 119. Italics are Lenin's.
[28] *Ibid.,* pp. 145, 161.
[29] *Ibid.,* p. 132.

(privileged officialdom, the chiefs of the standing army), the majority itself can directly fulfill all these functions, and the more the functions of state power devolve upon the people as a whole the less need is there for the existence of this power.[30]

With the disappearance of the state, as Lenin sees it, "an organization for the systematic use of *violence* by one class against the other, by one section of the population against another," will have disappeared also. Indeed, the development of socialism into communism means precisely that "the need for violence . . . will vanish altogether since people will *become accustomed* to observing the elementary conditions of social life *without violence* and *without subordination*." [31]

Fifty years of hindsight make it easy to disregard Lenin's insistence that his account of "the direct and immediate task of the revolutionary proletariat" is "not utopia" since grounded in the experience of the Commune.[32] Indeed, in retrospect, it is almost impossible to understand how a perceptive and fiercely probing social analyst such as Lenin could link this disclaimer of utopianism with a serious proposal of the German postal system of the seventies as a model of the revolutionary alternative to "the bureaucratic machine of the modern state." [33] But let us be careful lest, in deriding, we ourselves be had in derision.[34] For it could be that, *dei providentia et hominum confusione,* the penultimate word belongs to Marx and Engels and, thus, also to

[30] *Ibid.,* p. 133. Italics are Lenin's.
[31] *Ibid.,* p. 166. Italics are Lenin's.
[32] *Ibid.,* p. 139.
[33] *Ibid.,* p. 140.
[34] The allusion is to Psalm 2:4.

125

Lenin. "France," they had all agreed, "is the land where, more than anywhere else, the historical struggles were each time fought out to a decision." [35] Recently, almost a century after the abortive Commune, France found herself once again on the threshold of decision. Students occupied the Odéon and, for the first time in its history, forced the closing of the Sorbonne. Workers left their factories and offices and, short of a general strike, brought the country to a virtual economic and administrative standstill. Although the workers drew away from the students almost as quickly as they had united with them, the barricades in the streets and the formidable pressure of the Communist dominated trade unions forced the President of the Republic to dissolve the National Assembly and to announce a national referendum in which the people would choose between a government under the leadership of the incumbent President Charles de Gaulle, and what the President himself, and others, have described as "Communist totalitarianism." [36] The actors in the revolutionary confrontation had changed; but the confrontation itself found the barricades dividing workers and peasants and students, on the one side, from army, police, and the entrenched power of the government, on the other. This upheaval may or may not be considered the beginning of the "third French revolution." But it would be a mistake to suppose that either

[35] So Engels, in the Introduction to the 3rd ed. of *The Eighteenth Brumaire:* "In the coming proletarian revolution, France may show herself to be the classic land of the class struggle to a finish"; so Lenin, in *The State and Revolution,* p. 125.

[36] An informative summary of these developments may be found in *The New York Times,* Sunday, June 16, 1968, section 1, and Monday, June 17, 1968.

the "de-proletarianization" of French workers through the unexpected viability of capitalism in the West or the achievements of Soviet power in the East has invalidated the Marxist-Leninist analysis of the significance of France for the problem of the relation between state power and revolutionary social change. In the West, Berlin and Berkeley and New York have joined Paris in signaling the displacement of the workers as the bearers of the vision and the dynamics of the classless society by new victims of powerlessness: the students, the black peoples, the urban and the rural poor. The power line, however, is drawn very much as it was at the time of the Commune, i.e., between the machinery of the state and the economically underprivileged and disillusioned masses. In the East, the Soviet Union is harassed within and without by what Barrington Moore has identified and analyzed as "the dilemma of power." [37] The dilemma is that under the pressures of political responsibility the aims and the methods of the people's revolution work against each other. The goals of the new society cannot wait upon methods that achieve them without compromise, and, in turn, the means required by immediate political decisions obstruct the goals to such a degree as to require the indefinite extension of the time of achievement as the price of adhering to the goals.[38] Moore shows that almost all of Lenin's hopes and expectations were disappointed. In industry, a centralized system of control by the workers did not lead to the reduction of inequalities in pay and the eventual achieve-

[37] Barrington Moore, *Soviet Politics—the Dilemma of Power* (Cambridge: Harvard University Press, 1950).

[38] *Ibid.*, chap. 3.

ment of full equality. In agriculture, large-scale cooperative farming has not replaced the small peasant proprietors. And internationally, a successful revolution in Russia has not only not "set afire the socialist revolution in Europe" but revived in a more intense way the fierce debate about socialism in one country as a prelude to world communism. "Yet," Moore declares, "these beliefs constituted a point of departure to which the Bolsheviks were to return in times of trouble." [39] But there was also the question of "the relationship between the new toilers' state and the rest of the world." [40] If the state should succumb to the pressures of hostile encirclement, the fate of the Commune would be repeated in a more tragic way. If the state should survive, the problems would be more complex and destined to bring on the agonizing dilemma of power. In either case, the Marxist-Leninist identification of the key problem raised by the impact of social change upon power and of power upon social change is correct. It is the problem posed for every revolution by the machinery of the state and for the state by the dynamics of revolution. In short, the state is at once the *locus* and the *focus* of the problem of power, because in the state the ideological and the operational levels of power meet.

Messianism, Humanization, and the Problem of Power

The state is at once the precondition and the predicament of revolutionary social change. No revolution as

[39] *Ibid.*, p. 58.
[40] *Ibid.*, pp. 86-87.

long as the state remains untransformed! No revolution because the state resists transformation! These are the critical net results of Lenin's clarification in theory and in experience of the relation between revolution and the state. We must now note Lenin's clarification of the relation between revolution and humanization. Having identified the framework as well as the focus of revolution by its Marxist-Leninist occasion, we may then be able to suggest how the focus and framework of a theology for revolution illuminate this occasion and are, in turn, illuminated by it.

The framework of revolution is humanistic. However much the dynamics of social change may be regarded as a condition of life in this world, the process is never automatic. It evokes human participation and is, in turn, affected by that participation. Indeed, it is man's participation in and responsibility for social change that makes of change a political as well as a social fact. Politics is at once the link between the social and the human significance of change, and the instrument through which change is directed towards and organized for human purposes. Human needs and hopes, human structures and goals, human frustration and fulfillment are at once the motivation and the criterion of social change. In a word, the dynamics of social change are man's way of overcoming the credibility gap between human nature and human destiny; between who man is and who he seeks and dreams to become; between the actual conditions and the ineluctable possibilities of his life.

Hannah Arendt has instructively shown that this way of looking at change is "modern," i.e., it dates from the

eighteenth century.[41] Whereas in antiquity the experience of change was the fateful experience of recurrence,
devoid of genuine novelty, the modern experience of
change is "inextricably bound up with the notion that
the course of history suddenly begins anew, that an
entirely new story, a story never known or told before
is about to unfold." [42] When this experience is joined
with another, namely, the experience of the "new" as a
"new birth of freedom," change has become revolutionary. Miss Arendt quotes Condorcet as summing up
what everybody knew at the time of the French Revolution—namely, that "the word 'revolutionary' can be
applied only to revolutions whose aim is freedom." [43]

The Marxist-Leninist understanding of revolution fits
Condorcet's prescription. But two important additions
were made. One was the coupling of equality with freedom, thereby making more explicit that the "new birth
of freedom" meant not merely a new society but a new
humanity. In his "Criticism of the Gotha Program,"
Marx had celebrated in anticipation

[41] Hannah Arendt, *On Revolution* (New York: Viking Press,
1963; 4th printing, 1967) . See esp. chaps. I, V, VI.

[42] *Ibid.,* p. 21. Miss Arendt also notes that Greek and Roman
responses to change did not entirely coincide. Of Polybius, she
writes that he "was perhaps the first writer to become aware of
the decisive factor of generations following one another through
history" and that he "looked upon Roman affairs with a Greek
eye when he pointed to this unalterable constant coming and
going in the realm of the political, although he knew it was the
business of Roman, as distinguished from Greek, education to
bind the 'new ones' to the old, to make the young worthy of their
ancestors." (P. 20.)

[43] *Ibid.,* p. 21. See Condorcet, *Sur le Sens du Mot Revolution-
naires, Oeuvres,* 1847-49, Vol. XII.

a higher phase of Communist society, after the enslaving subordination of the individual to the division of labor shall have disappeared, and with it the antagonism between intellectual and manual labor, after labor has become not only a means of life but also the primary necessity of life; when, with the development of the individual in every sense, the productive forces also increase and all the springs of collective wealth flow with abundance—only then . . . can society inscribe upon its banner: "From each according to his abilities, to each according to his needs!" [44]

Consistent with his clarification of Marx's vision and analysis at the operational level, Lenin declares that:

Democracy means equality. The great significance of the proletariat's struggle for equality and of equality as a slogan will be clear if we correctly interpret it as meaning the abolition of classes. But democracy means only *formal* equality. And as soon as equality is achieved for all members of society *in relation* to ownership of the means of production, that is equality of labor and equality of wages, humanity will inevitably be confronted with the question of advancing farther, from formal equality to actual equality, i.e., to the realization of the rule "from each according to his ability to each according to his needs." By what stages, by means of what practical measures humanity will proceed to this supreme aim—we do not and cannot know. [45]

The other important addition to Condorcet's prescription for revolution was the Marxist-Leninist concentration upon the economic matrix of freedom and equality. In this way, the relation between revolution and human-

[44] Karl Marx,"The Criticism of the Gotha Program," in *Capital, the Communist Manifesto, and Other Writings* (New York: Modern Library, 1932) , p. 7.
[45] *The State and Revolution*, p. 180.

ization achieved concrete historical expression. Lenin had already foreshadowed this concern in his repudiation of the idolatry of the anarchists.[46] In that connection, he had given a quick rundown of the humanistic conditions for revolution in concrete socioeconomic terms. He had spoken of "the conditions of great social changes," of "the creative power of revolution," of "the concrete lessons of earlier proletarian revolutions," and of the "practical conditions of the mass movement." To ask what is *humanistic* about these conditions is to overlook or to fail to understand the vision and passion for the human in every decisive struggle to achieve a new beginning. To ask what is *humanistic* about these conditions is to overlook or fail to understand what, beyond success or failure, remains as the great achievement of Lenin in the theory and practice of revolution. This achievement is his unyielding effort to give operational effectiveness to Marx's insistence upon the human significance of work (labor) and upon the historical and economic conditions for realizing this human significance. When his own turn came to face with and for the sake of humanity the question of advancing from formal to actual equality, Lenin proceeded with an almost fanatical combination of pragmatism and agnosticism. Since the dialectical goal of history was the humanization of man in society, he risked both acting as an opportunist and being misunderstood as an opportunist in taking decisions required by an open-ended and uncertain way ahead. The decision-making exhibited

[46] *Ibid.*, p. 7.

nothing so much as what Barrington Moore has called "a double paradox." He writes:

Lenin and his followers set out to achieve for humanity the goals of freedom and equality by means of an organization that denied these same principles. It was anticipated that the denial would be temporary and that the fruits of victory would bring the goals desired. Instead, discipline, authority, and inequality had to be intensified after victory.[47]

The paradox, of course, spells historical and revolutionary failure. But does the failure mean that Bakunin and Trotsky were right after all?[48] On the contrary, it means failure in the grand tradition. Just as Augustine, long ago, had declared that men never make war for the sake of war but always for the sake of peace,[49] so Lenin shows that men engage in revolution not for the sake of revolution but for the sake of humanization. Lenin's failure confirms rather than invalidates his analysis. The clarification of the relation between revolution and humanization and the relation between revolution and the state exposes the crucial importance of the problem of

[47] Moore, *Soviet Politics—the Dilemma of Power,* pp. 81-82.

[48] Bakunin vigorously opposed Marx on the role of the state, even in an intermediate role. He wanted a "free federation of all kinds of workers' associations liberated from the yoke of the state." See his letter to the internationalists of the Romagna, January 28, 1872, quoted by Otto Ruehle, *Karl Marx* (New York: Viking Press, 1929), pp. 290 ff. Trotsky vigorously fought against what he called the "bureaucratic decentralization" in Lenin's program, and Stalin's following after, and he steadily moved toward a categorical either:or—either international revolution, or the abandonment of the socialist experiment in Russia. See Moore, *Soviet Politics,* p. 102.

[49] Augustine, *City of God,* Bk. XIX, 13.

power for the humanization of man, and thus also for a theory of revolution.

The problem of power is the problem of giving effective human shape to the humanizing purpose and direction of the revolutionary dynamics of social change. As Lenin's analysis has shown, this includes ideological and operational factors which come to a critical focus in the instrumentality of the state.[50] The state is the decisive link between perspective and policy in the humanizing control and consequences of power. The state can either make room for or make impossible—in Hannah Arendt's moving phrase—"the space of men's free deeds and living words which could endow life with splendor." [51]

By a curious riddle of history, the state is the locus and focus of the problem of power, not only for a *theory of revolution* but also for a *theology for revolution*. Thus, the point at which the ideological and operational levels of power meet is also the point at which Marxism and Christianity meet. Both Marxism and Christianity have been brought, by reason of their common participation in the dynamics of social change and their separate histories of response to the impact of social change upon power and of power upon social change, to an identical *kairos*, i.e., an identical moment of truth and new be-

[50] Raymond Aron's suggestion that the disintegration of the nation-state on the nineteenth-century European model and its replacement by ethnocentric in contrast to class politics does not alter the instrumental relation of the state to power, because the sociological shift from class to race or nationality does not alter the economic basis of power. See Harvery Wheeler, fellow of the Center for the Study of Democratic Institutions, in The *Saturday Review*, Vol. LI, no. 24 (June 15, 1968) , p. 20.

[51] *On Revolution*, p. 285.

ginning. Such a moment is always a moment of reciprocal illumination among its formative participants, freeing them for the correction of dogmatisms and obscurantisms, for a fresh assessment of mistakes and possibilities, and for a renewing openness to the advent of transfiguration exactly at those boundaries that mark the difference between the end of the beginning and the beginning of the end.

The moment of truth and new beginning concerns the point at which and from which the referent, the context, the process, and the power of humanization occur. Each in its own way, Marxism and Christianity have drawn a blank exactly at the point at which the problem of power shatters the power of revolution to achieve humanization. Both Marxism and Christianity have come to grief in dealing with the state. Marxists seek to arbitrarily limit the role of the state to its ideologically determined function as the instrument of class exploitation that must disappear by definition when the classless society appears. Christians seek to arbitrarily limit the role of the state to its ideologically determined function as the instrument of order against chaos, of authority against anarchy, "not a terror to good conduct, but to bad" (Rom. 13:3), superfluous only in the life of the world to come. Both Marxists and Christians have a considerable backlog of experience and evidence to share with each other, for instruction and correction, if they are to transcend the frustrating utopianism and the resigned pessimism that have hitherto defeated their respective attempts to deal with power and have made them enemies. If Marxists and Christians should somehow begin to face together the blunt reality of power, they might find themselves on the way toward an ideological and operational transfiguration safely beyond apostasy and idolatry, both religious and secular. Marxists can teach Christians that the power of the state, however purposeful it may be, is operationally exposed to dehumanizing corruption, so pervasive and enervating as to make its imminent expendability a demand of justice and freedom. Christians can teach Marxists that the power of the state, however corrupt it may be, is operationally purposeful, lest the demand for justice and freedom be deprived of the reverence and reconciliation without which, hydra-like, they spawn their opposites. How, then, shall Marxist deeds and Christian words be transfigured so as to transfigure also Marxist words and Christian deeds? By what power shall the humanizing thrust of revolutionary sensitivity and insight be restored from semantic legerdemain (which is apostasy) to its transforming purpose? By what power shall the humanizing thrust of revolutionary sensitivity and insight be restored from the self-justifying satisfaction of simplistic immediacy (which is idolatry) to its transforming purpose? If it should turn out that the mystery of history, by which and within which Christians and Marxists have been drawn together, is a sign of the secret of history, which Marxists and Christians are required to explore together by the urgency of the problem of power upon which the humanization of man in history has come to grief, there could be a liberating and integrating answer to these questions.

The urgency of the questions and the urgency of the problem point to the possibility of a fresh examination of the ideological and operational reality and effectiveness of the power by which the mystery of history is indeed a sign of the secret of history. This power is the power of a messianic presence through whom the humanization of men in history is carried out from its beginning to its end. A messianic presence is a historical presence whose renewing power begins with the freedom of a binding commitment and functions with enlarging inclusiveness as *the* power of renewal of man in himself and in his communities. Messianism is the historicization of the human through the experience of confrontation by and response to the bearer in his person of the presence and power of "the Author and Giver of felicity" who "Himself gives earthly kingdoms both to good and bad." [52] Christians find in Marxists a messianic people without a Messiah. Marxists find in Christians a commitment to a messianic presence, but no messianic people. For Marxists, the Messiah is absent and unnecessary; for Christians, he is hidden and without power in the world. Humanization is the transfiguration of the historical through the experience of freedom from self-justifying ends and means, motivations, and structures, and of freedom for fulfilling participation in the human shape of things to come. Christians find in Marxists a self-justifying self-identity that cannot bring together the vision that informs its passion and the policies its passion seeks. Marxists find in Christians a self-justifying avoidance of the risk of being justified by faith that hankers more for the fleshpots of Egypt than it hungers for the promised land. For Marxists, power is consumed

[52] Augustine, *City of God,* Bk. IV, 33.

137

by the fury of recrimination. For Christians, power is ultimately consumed by the failure of reconciliation. In either case, the bearing of the relation between messianism and humanization upon the fact and the dynamics of social change has lost the referent, context, process, and power in terms of which the humanization of the historical can surmount the problem of power. The transfiguration of power waits upon the power of transfiguration. If Christians and Marxists can begin to explore together their present experience in the light of these perspectives, it may be given to them also to discover together "by what stages, by means of what practical measures humanity will proceed to this supreme aim." Meanwhile, as Lenin also said, "we do not know and cannot know." But messianic sensitivity and seeking are preceded, accompanied, and followed by a promise and a way of fulfillment. We can join up with "Joshua the son of Nun and Caleb the son of Jephunneh," who were among those who had spied out the land, rent their clothes, and said to all the people of [the promise],

"The land, which we passed through to spy it out, is an exceedingly good land. If the Lord delights in us, he will bring us into this land and give it to us, a land which flows with milk and honey. Only, do not rebel against the Lord; and do not fear the people of the land, for they are bread for us; and their protection is removed from them, and the Lord is with us; do not fear them."

Then the glory of the Lord appeared at the tent of meeting to all the people of [the promise]. And the Lord said . . . "but truly, as I live, and as all the earth shall be filled with the glory of the Lord, none of the men who have seen my glory and my signs which I wrought in Egypt and in the wilderness, and yet have put me to the proof . . . and have not hearkened to my voice, shall see the land which I swore to give to their fathers; and none of those who despised me shall see it. But my servant Caleb, because he has a different spirit and has followed me fully, I will bring into the land into which he went, and his descendants shall possess it." [53]

[53] Num. 14:6-11, 20-24 RSV. The phrase "people of the promise" has been substituted for the phrase "people of Israel," which appears in the text.

The Changing Character of Communism

SIDNEY LENS

No issue affects our nation or, for that matter, our individual lives as decisively as communism. A half-century after the Russian Revolution, it is still the overriding factor in international relations. To contain communism and to roll it back, our own country has spent $900,000,000,000 on its military establishment since the end of the war. This is a staggering expenditure, which, if used otherwise, would have replaced every slum home in the nation, solved our water problem, provided 600,000 schoolrooms, 1,000,000 hospital beds, and many other of our social needs, leaving at least $15,000,000,000 to $20,000,000,000 a year for economic aid to the developing nations. If, then, communism is changing, it is urgent for us to know in what way, why, and how it affects the prospect for world peace. Against this background of change we can assess our past strategy to see if we have calculated correctly or incorrectly, as well as evolve a new approach tailored to the circumstances.

The conventional wisdom of the past two decades has held that communism has within it certain innate characteristics with which we in the so-called free world cannot compromise. Even now, when there are at least five distinct brands and an obvious polycentric trend in the Communist world, the stereotype we fashioned for ourselves continues to haunt us. We note changes in some of their economies in the direction of what we call liberalism, and changes in their rhetoric that in another day they themselves would have called class collaborationist. But there remains immutable in our national mind the stereotype of a communism that is essentially changeless and that must be removed from the scene if our own society is to flourish.

Our stereotype is of the Soviet Union in the quarter of a century when Joseph Stalin ruled it. We think of the purge trials of the 1930's which claimed almost all the original Bolshevik leaders—Zinoviev, Kamenev, Bukharin, Rakovsky, Radek, and, at long distance by assassination, Leon Trotsky. We think of the millions incarcerated in forced labor camps, the midnight knock, the emasculation of unions and free speech, the rigid domination of the economy, the sacrifice of so many individuals in the interests of the state, the terrible secret police, the paucity of consumer goods and housing facilities, and, above all, the rhetoric of revolution for the rest of the world. It is around this stereotype that we

141

Americans have accepted the strategy of the Cold War. We have concluded, with a considerable amount of prodding by our military-industrial complex, that communism is not merely an enemy, but a permanent enemy. In the final analysis, we say, it is either "communism" or "freedom" that will survive; the two systems cannot coexist indefinitely, competitively or otherwise. Our military and political leaders have built hundreds of military bases around the world to encircle the Communist nations, hold them in check for the moment, until—hopefully—the moment arrives when communism can be rolled back and destroyed. Our forty thousand megatons of hydrogen bombs—equal to twelve or thirteen tons of dynamite for every man, woman, and child in the world; our chemical, bacterial, and radiological weapons; our many military treaties; our intervention in Vietnam, Thailand, the Dominican Republic, and elsewhere, are all part of this strategy. And since the conflict is viewed as a permanent one, to the bitter end, each war or military confrontation—be it Berlin, Korea, or Vietnam—is considered simply a skirmish in a greater war.

A few years ago I had a talk with Secretary of Defense Robert McNamara's top assistant about fallout shelters. I argued that civil defense in the final analysis would not save any lives, even assuming that the shelters were effective per se, because the Russians would react to them by building new weapons and taking other steps to circumvent our advantage. The assistant, to my surprise, conceded the point: fallout shelters in the long run would save no lives. But his rationale for building them was most revealing. "If we build such shelters," he said, "the Russians will have to spend enormous additional sums counteracting us. In doing so they will have to withdraw resources from their economy and reduce the amount of consumer products for their people. They will have to lower living standards and thereby create mass disaffection. What," he asked, "is wrong with that?" I can think of many things wrong with that, not the least of which is that it is immoral and deceptive. But what is significant is the thinking behind it, of an eternal war between two social systems that cannot find a modus vivendi. The assumption is implicit that no matter how communism changes—and the assistant to McNamara readily admitted it was changing—there will always be at its hard core a basic character with which we cannot compromise. President Truman expressed it in simplistic terms when, in proclaiming the Truman Doctrine back in 1947, he said that freedom means free enterprise, and any system that does not accept free enterprise must be viewed as an enemy of the United States.

In the face of this type of rigidity it would be wise for us, it seems to me, to move beyond the passions of the Cold War to put communism in a proper historical context. To begin with, it is necessary to note that for most of man's existence on this planet he has lived under a system of communism—common ownership of property. It is only with the dawn of what we call civilization that private and individual ownership of the means of production begins to emerge. Secondly, the theory of communism is older as a religious doctrine than as a secular doctrine. Hundreds of years before Karl Marx, medieval monks were debating its virtues;

143

and long before that, according to the socialist philosopher Karl Kautsky in his *Foundations of Christianity*, the early Christians preached and practiced communism. Kautsky claims that the followers of Christ were greatly influenced by the Essenes, a Judaic order that lived in common dwellings, four thousand strong, and shared both property and work. The communistic theme—again according to Kautsky—is repeated in the Acts of the Apostles: "And all who believed were together and had all things in common; and they sold their possessions and goods and distributed them to all, as any had need" (Acts 2:44-45 RSV). There is little difference between this and the words in the *Communist Manifesto* of Marx and Engels: "From each according to his ability, to each according to his needs." Similar sentiments were expressed by John in his eleventh homily on the Acts of the Apostles: "Grace was among them, since nobody suffered want, that is, since they gave so willingly that no one remained poor. For they did not give a part, keeping another part for themselves; they gave everything in their possession" (Acts 4:33-35). Kautsky claims further that the first Christians actually lived on a communistic plan, with the bishop as their treasurer, and the "purse," so often referred to, as the common purse for all.

Moving to the Middle Ages we find the monks arguing not that communism is an evil system—on the contrary they conceded it was the *natural order* of things—but that man was too greedy to enjoy it. Religious groups, however, have often returned to a communistic way of life. Dissenting sects of the seventeenth and eighteenth centuries, such as the Diggers, the Levellers, the Anabaptists, a wing of the Society of Friends (Quakers), preached communism and on occasion formed communist communities. We find many of them in America —the Shakers, for instance—during the first two and a half centuries in our own nation's history. One such group, the Oneida Perfectionists, believed in communism not only in property relationships but also in sex. The Brook Farm experiment, which included some of the greatest writers in American history—Emerson, Hawthorne, George Ripley—was a communist experiment, as were the communities established by followers of Robert Owen, Horace Greeley, and Albert Brisbane during the first half of the nineteenth century.

I mention all of this not because these older religious and utopian forms of communism are necessarily similar in doctrinal roots to the communism of Marx, Lenin, Stalin, and Mao, but solely to indicate that the word is not a scourge, as the propaganda of the Cold War would tend to indicate. Many decent, even noble, people have believed throughout history in the idea of total sharing, brotherhood, communal ownership. These principles were still adhered to among many tribes in Africa and elsewhere until recently and may still be in vogue in some places. With all the incursion of city life and the capitalist marketplace, friends in Nairobi, Kenya, and Leopoldville, Belgian Congo, told me a few years ago that a tribesman can be away from his village ten or twenty years and, on returning, still be given a patch of land from the tribe's holding.

When we turn now from older communisms to Marxist communism, what is so surprising is not the changelessness of both theory and practice, but its constant and invariable *proclivity* to change—as if it were operating on its own dialectic. Certainly there are a few basic themes, such as historical materialism, the class struggle, the theory of surplus value, which are accepted as gospel by all Communists. But beyond that it is just as fallacious to equate all of Marxian communism and its fifty-seven varieties with the stereotype of Stalinism, as it would be to equate Christianity with the practices of the Black Popes, or to fail to distinguish between the capitalism of the United States and that of Portugal. The fact is that communism has always been a changing phenomenon, in strategy as well as doctrine.

Consider its historical evolution. As Marx saw it, communism would arrive first in those countries that were industrially advanced, where there had already been a considerable accumulation of capital, a strong infrastructure, and where the transition from capitalism to communism could be executed with the least strain. In Britain and the United States he foresaw the possibility that this changeover could take place without violent uprising, simply through the ballot box. What Marx did, in a sense, was add to the religious rationale for communism a historical and economic basis. In the ensuing years there were great arguments between Marx and Bakunin, between the Marxians and the Lassalleans, between the Bernstein "revisionists" and the revolutionaries, between Kautsky and Liebknecht, over how the transformation could come about. During the first World War the schism between those who supported their own countries and those who espoused an international general strike or international revolution was so great that the Second International disintegrated.

Marx's scenario for revolution, it turned out early in

this century, was not realistic and had to be modified by Lenin. The revolution, when it did occur, came not to an advanced capitalist nation but to capitalism's "weakest link," Russia, with a strong feudal carryover. Lenin, in leading this revolution, modified the Marxian strategy and theory perceptibly. He and Trotsky were authors of a thesis that there could be a revolution that combined both the bourgeois and proletarian phases. This was a dramatic departure, it must be noted, from the standard notion of historical materialism, in which capitalism came first, matured through a process of birth, growth, and decay, to be replaced in due time by the dictatorship of the proletariat. Lenin and Trotsky believed these two phases could be telescoped into a single period and guided their revolution in that direction.

Parenthetically, it is useful to record the acclaim received by the Bolshevik Revolution of 1917 in the United States, if only to indicate there was a time when attitudes were more flexible. "Thank God for the Russian Revolution," exclaimed churchman Dr. John Haynes Holmes, expressing a sentiment that was echoed by thousands of other liberal clergymen. All wings of the Socialist Party, right to left and including the moderate *Jewish Daily Forward,* hailed the revolution. Among its supporters were Norman Thomas, Roger Baldwin, and the well-known muckraker Lincoln Steffens, who said he had seen the future "and it works." Eugene V. Debs, Socialist presidential candidate, said he was a Bolshevik to the tips of his toes. Innumerable liberals greeted the revolution as one of history's greatest liberating events. That many were to change their opinions does not alter the fact that the communism they first saw was very much

147

different from the stereotype we currently adhere to.

Leninist communism, it must be pointed out, differed markedly from the Stalinist form. To begin with, it permitted two opposition parties to exist for a while, the left wings of the Mensheviks and Social Revolutionaries. When, after an attempt was made to assassinate Lenin, the opposition was dissolved, wide-scale factionalism continued within the Bolshevik Party, both temporary and permanent factions, each publishing its own bulletins and carrying articles of its views into the official press. From 1917 to 1924 one is struck by the bewildering change in political lineups and the bitter—and legal—polemics within Bolshevik ranks. Prior to the seizure of power, when Lenin first returned to Russia, most of the leadership of the Party—including Stalin, Zinoviev, and Kamenev—opposed Lenin's view that a "proletarian revolution" was the order of the day. On the eve of the uprising of November 7, Zinoviev and Kamenev bitterly assailed the idea of the Bolsheviks making a revolution on their own. Subsequent to the seizure of power a three-cornered contest broke out within the Central Committee of the Party over the question of peace with Germany. Bukharin, leader of the majority wing, favored a military defense and continued war; Trotsky called for a policy of neither war nor peace, waiting it out; Lenin, at the head of the smallest faction, favored coming to terms with the Germans immediately and withdrawing from the war. During the following years vigorous debates and faction fights ensued over such questions as the role of trade unions during the 1918-20 Civil War, workers' control of the factories, the role of the Communist Party, and many other issues. The stereotype of a monolithic force permitting no discussion on penalty of arrest or execution was not in evidence. Considering the shocking state of the Soviet economy, after a war in which the nation had suffered ten million casualties and ninety percent of the industry and railroads had been put out of comission, it is remarkable that this much dissent was tolerated.

A second point to be noted in this early period of the Soviet republic was programmatic flexibility. The Bolshevik program, in the abstract, called for national ownership of the land. In practice this should have translated itself into the organization of large state farms and collectives. But Lenin did not choose to implement his own program; instead he put into force that of the Social Revolutionaries calling for *individual* farms. The first decree of the Bolsheviks after gaining the helm in 1917 was to divide the land, giving peasants the right to operate their own plots. Flexibility was also evident in other areas. During the Civil War the state took over total direction of the economy, abolishing all private enterprise. When the war was over it introduced the New Economic Policy, permitting a considerable area where private entrepreneurs could function and earn a profit. The first impulse was to permit the workers of each factory to control their own operation. This was later changed so that "workers' control of production," a key Bolshevik slogan, was taken to mean worker supervision over the whole economy as a planned unit. Whether this was more or less beneficial for the laboring class is beside the point; what is significant is the changeability of communism in the face of circumstances: the first method didn't work, so it was changed. In those formative years, too, it should be emphasized, strikes were tolerated, and prices were permitted to find their own level on the market—what we now call "liberalized" communism.

The metamorphosis from Leninism to Stalinism is usually viewed as an inevitable transition, as if Stalinism were already inherent in Leninism, only waiting to come to full flower. This, too, does not, it seems to me, accord with the facts. If there is one thing in the character of communism that stands out, it is that its forms are vitally affected by international relationships and international pressures. We do not know what type of communism would have emerged predominant if the Allies had not decided to send fourteen armies to the Soviet Union in 1918, or if they had not underwritten the military efforts of the counterrevolutionary White Guards. There were people such as William C. Bullitt and Lincoln Steffens who pleaded with the United States to come to terms with the Communists instead of trying to isolate them. Bullitt and Steffens had been dispatched by President Wilson to arrange an understanding with Lenin and Trotsky, and both came back with what they considered a highly favorable proposal. Yet Wilson refused to discuss the proposal, and by this time public opinion was so poisoned that Prime Minister Lloyd George of Britain told the two emissaries that any kind of modus vivendi was out of the question. Instead of coexistence the West pursued the policy of military rollback, and when that failed, isolation. Secretary of State Bainbridge Colby stated in 1920 that the United States could not recognize the Soviet Union because it was committed to revolution, exactly the argument that had been used by the Russian

Czar after the American Revolution when Russia refused to recognize the United States for thirty-three years. Instead of cooperation and trade, the West placed a cordon sanitaire around the Soviets, forged a Little Entente, and refused them any long-term credits to rebuild their territory.

For a nation whose economy had been reduced from a gross national product of seven billion rubles in 1913 to one and one-third billion in 1920, isolation imposed severe hardships. Initially the Bolsheviks were of the opinion that such handicaps could be overcome when the more advanced Germany turned to Bolshevism. But when the German, Hungarian, and other revolutions failed from 1917 to 1924, and when the radical wave had receded, an inevitable dispute broke out in Communist ranks as to how to proceed.

One faction, led by Bukharin, favored continuing the policy of slow industrialization and slow improvement of living standards. The Soviet Union was then accumulating capital at the rate of 7 to 9 percent of its GNP. That meant that for every dollar of national product 91 to 93 percent remained for consumption. The workers and peasants, whose standards had gone up appreciably since 1921, could continue to expect additional benefits. Trotsky's views were somewhat more complicated. Unless the city factories were able to make available consumer goods to the farmers, he said, the latter would soon stop bringing their grain to the market. It was urgent therefore to significantly increase capital formation to 17 percent so as to build the plants to provide finished goods. The additional money could be raised by levying much higher taxes on the middle and upper peasants. This would permit the country to spend 83 cents of every dollar of production for consumption.

Stalin, when he became unchallenged master of the Soviet Union, followed a much more sanguine course. Unlike Trotsky he had little faith in "proletarian revolutions" breaking out elsewhere. Where Trotsky had urged the Communists to "go it alone" in China, Stalin promulgated the concept of a "bloc of four classes" and collaboration with Chiang Kai-shek. In Stalin's view in 1929, the Soviet Union was on the verge of being attacked by the capitalist world, and efforts must therefore be made immediately to build a heavy industry on which to sustain a military machine. To accomplish this Stalin instituted a rate of capital formation of 33 percent, which meant that of every dollar of production only 67 cents was left for consumption. Thus, while the Soviet Union was exporting grain and sugar its people were going without these commodities, or with curtailed amounts, at home. Furthermore, to export the grain it was necessary that the peasant bring it to market. But since, as Trotsky had predicted, there was little to buy in the cities, the peasant was withholding it. To collect the grain, therefore, Stalin formed collective farms, forcing the individualistic peasant into a collective community he did not want to enter. The peasant reacted by killing off his cattle—it took the Soviets a quarter of a century to recover from this loss—and by staging at least 150 peasant rebellions. Stalin's answer, without going into details, was greatly to enlarge the secret police and institute a reign of terror against the recalcitrants. Many were killed and many more jailed, but in the end the countryside was in the secret police's hands. Similarly in the cities, as living standards dropped and workers went on strike, the walkouts were smashed by police and a rigid regimen was imposed on the laborers. The objective of rapid capital accumulation and heavy industry, however, was achieved. Prior to collectivization the state was able to buy ten million tons of grain from the peasants each year; afterwards it *exacted* twenty-five million tons. And, as we know from the oft-repeated statistics of the five-year plans, heavy industry grew by leaps and bounds.

Here, we have the background for Stalinism. It evolved not as something inherent in Communist theory, but as the result of the exigencies and pressures of isolation. One thing led to another. Failure to negotiate long-term credits made it necessary to "squeeze" the peasants and workers in order to form capital. Squeezing resulted in a reactive opposition. Opposition led to a vast expansion of the police forces, and repression. Fear of war caused the Stalinists to accelerate heavy industry production; acceleration led to a lopsided economy. While big factories were being built few new apartments were rising. Real wages, for a considerable period, fell. The worker chafed at the bit, and the state retaliated by imprisoning the malcontents and those who came late to work or were unduly absent. Since there was a shortage of everything, the government rigidly controlled all prices, abolished the market mechanism, and imposed controls over every minor facet of the economy. When all these restrictions proved harshly burdensome the next phase of the drama unfolded. Though there no longer were any factions permitted for fear of mass uprising, discussion and opposition were still tolerated *within* the

Central Committee after the exile of Trotsky. But when it became obvious that disaffection might result in a test for power—perhaps around the Leningrad leader Kirov, who was assassinated in 1934—this form of dissent, too, was made illegal. The circle had been squared, from the dictatorship of the proletariat to the dictatorship of the party to the dictatorship of the secret police and one man. Oskar Lange in Warsaw told me many years later how the secret police controlled the Communist leadership and how in turn it was controlled by Stalin. The second in command of this agency was always someone who reported directly to Stalin and was not under the discipline of the head man. The Soviet dictator, therefore, always had his finger on potential revolt. As for the members of the government, the secret police prepared indictments for possible use against all of them, and when any threatened to kick the traces they were confronted with the "charges" and warned that unless they followed the Stalinist policy they would be put on trial. The "evidence" of course, was fabricated, but it didn't matter since the organs of justice were also in Stalin's hands.

This, then, was the most extreme form of communism —totalitarianism. It lasted a long time, but one must see it as part of a process, and from our point of view as part of the interplay between communism and capitalism. I doubt if this extreme form would have emerged had it not been for the severity of Western attitudes—a view I believe is shared by George F. Kennan. If the course of communism is described in terms of popular decision-making rights, we find a reel pulling in tight and tighter, then slowly unreeling, consonant with economic and political realities, as well as with the virtues and vices of some of its leaders. The revolution itself undoubtedly had a large popular base and was greeted with enthusiasm, but in the following decade the area of popular decision narrowed perceptibly and, with the coming of Stalinism, disappeared. Since the death of Stalin in 1953, and with the enormous recovery and growth of Soviet economic strength, the process is being reversed. Despite the Cold War the Soviets feel more secure, and their land is certainly more affluent. In this condition repressive features are disappearing and—hesitantly—certain positive rights are being won. The purge trials are a thing of the past, the forced labor regime is gone, the sizable increase in consumer goods has resulted in a considerable improvement in living standards, the economy now supports not only heavy industry but a very large program for apartment building. The individual can today challenge his union, his superior, and his state in a way he could not before. I spoke with workers in the Soviet Union, for instance, who were taking their plant management to court because they were not being allocated apartments promised them. Such a step in Stalin's day would have led to immediate arrest. Workers can now change jobs, come in late, or be absent, again without police measures being taken against them. With the institution of economic "Libermanism" both plant supervisors and workers are being given a larger say in planning production and enjoying its benefits. This is not yet nirvana, but it is a long way from the terrifying life under Stalin, and what's more, it is a condition that is irreversible. The Soviet Union is now a "have" country, with a gross national product somewhere between three hundred and five hundred billion dollars, about where the United States was ten or fifteen years ago.

As a "have" country Russia reacts to political and economic realities in a very much different way than when it was a "have-not" nation. Take the question of foreign policy: Apart from its memory of two terrifying wars and the havoc wrought by them, the Soviet Union now has much more to lose in case of hostilities. A half-century after the revolution, therefore, its policy is "softer," geared toward finding a way of competitive coexistence. Lenin told the Communist International in 1919, "We do not need an agreement with the bourgeoisie, we are going into the last decisive fight with it." But in 1962 Khrushchev said that war can be banished "before the complete victory of socialism on earth, with capitalism surviving in part of the world." The Soviets of course still want to see a world made up entirely of leftist nations (just as the United States would like to see a world made up entirely of pro-capitalist nations), but they rely primarily on popular fronts, trade, contact, and elections as their major weapons. This is not merely a pose, it is part of their political necessity. And when on occasion, such as in Vietnam, the Soviets do support a war of national liberation that is violent, it is not necessarily of their own choosing, for if they failed to aid it they would lose their total international following.

Or, take the internal economy of the Soviet Union. There was a time when Soviet production could be increased helter-skelter simply by pouring in additional manpower no matter how inefficient. Since the resources of manpower in the villages were towering, this presented little problem. Now, however, if production is to be increased the main reliance must be on the rise in productivity by each individual worker. If the individual worker is truly to become more productive, however, he must be relieved of fear and he must be given certain rewards. Hence the vast campaign for housing, the improvement of transportation service, the increase in wages, the shortening of hours, the relaxation of repression.

The corollaries of this change, of course, are monumental. They require change in the legal and penal system, abolition of forced labor, greater freedom for intellectual expression, and more rights for the artists, despite some of the imprisonments of those considered to be "too liberal." To produce more consumer goods the state must tap the initiative at the grass roots—the plant manager, for instance—rather than impose a plan from on top, from Moscow. Thus the "free market"—which our propagandists falsely call a partial return to capitalism—comes back into use in many industries as a corrective to bad planning. And since the state's hold over the individual is loosening *within* the Soviet Union, its Communist Party cannot exercise the same domination over Communist parties elsewhere. The pressures it once used to bring them into line, stern and harsh, can no longer be applied. A relaxation at home leads to polycentrism abroad, not so much on doctrinal as on pragmatic grounds.

This polycentrism is matched by independent tendencies within the Communist world that began to be visible long before Stalin's death. It began, in fact, in the late twenties and thirties when in far-off China Mao Tse-tung refused to accept the Stalinist order to concentrate on the city proletariat as his cadre for revolution, but in violation of that order based himself on peasant guerrillas in the villages. Again, after the war, Mao refused to follow Stalin's instructions to join a popular front government under Chiang Kai-shek. It is now documented from many sources that he decided instead to move straight ahead toward seizure of power, a task which he accomplished in 1949. The tendency toward independence was also evident elsewhere in the Far East. Tan Malaka in Indonesia broke away from the Stalinist monolith to build an independent Communist Party. (Adam Malik, the recent foreign minister of that country, was once an adherent of it.) In Indochina Ho Chiminh produced a nationalist program that showed many independent characteristics. In India there were four Communist Parties—two "soft," two "hard." In Burma, the hard Red Flag Communists challenged the softer White Flag Communists.

The first significant structural break in world communism occurred in Yugoslavia, where Tito withdrew from the monolith in 1948 in protest against Soviet interference in his internal affairs. If the difference between Stalinism and Titoism originally was small in the doctrinal and strategical areas it ultimately grew wide as a chasm. Tito introduced three new concepts—self-management, profitability, decentralism—which made Titoism as dramatically different from Stalinist communism as U.S. capitalism is from that of Spain. In the typical Yugoslav factory the workers, in addition to electing a union committee to handle their job grievances, select a workers council, which in turn chooses a management committee. This latter has veto power in hiring the plant manager, price and production policies, and all the normal decisions of management. Its task is to assure a profit, and because a sizable part of that profit goes to the workers they obviously have a stake in the decisions that are made. Furthermore, each department is operated as an enclosed unit, with the workers of that department permitted to do their own hiring and firing collectively and arrange their own production schedules. They are paid on the basis of the profitability of their department, just as if they were owners, though, of course, the major portion of the profit goes to the state.

The system is actually much more complex, but what is significant here is its results. Cut off from the umbilicus of Russia, Tito had to find his own economic way. He chose this economic pattern of self-management and profitability. To make it effective, however, he had to assure that workers would exercise their initiative; otherwise the system would collapse. But if initiative is the desired goal the workers must not be afraid to express themselves. From this attitude many far-reaching changes follow. The League of Communists, for one thing, must stop injecting itself into every decision, acting as a centralized monolith. The workers must be permitted to elect the men they deem best to the management committee, whether Communists or not. Each factory must have a degree of autonomy in formulating its production plan, and the national planning agency must become less a master than a coordinating force. Decentralism, at least to an extent, must become a guiding motif throughout the nation, local and provincial bodies gaining considerably more prerogatives than previously. And if the worker is to have an incentive for being more efficient and improving "profitability" he must have an opportunity to secure better housing and consumer goods. The first time I was in Yugoslavia, in 1950, I recall that it was impossible to buy a needle in the leading stores. I saw illiterate farmers buying filing cabinets when put on sale because there was little else to purchase with their money. On succeeding trips to Yugoslavia conditions changed drastically, with consumer goods and housing becoming ever more available. Furthermore, a system that caters to initiative and efficiency sometimes finds itself with redundant laborers on its hands. It must either pay them unemployment compensation or permit them to travel out of the country for jobs; and if the unemployed are permitted to leave, the nation cannot keep its employed locked behind closed borders. It must permit them, too, to travel to other countries during their holidays or to seek work. This so-called liberalization does not lead to capitalism, for the state continues to own the means of production, but it leads to an entirely different form of planning and an entirely different attitude toward personal liberty than existed under Stalinism. Again, it is not abstract doctrine but economic pragmatism that leads to change.

One can argue that such changes mean little, that the essence of communism is still the same, that there is no democracy in Yugoslavia—in our two-party sense—that people like Djilas were held in jail for expressing libertarian views. But none of these points, it seems to me, has validity. "Democracy," too, is not an abstract and formless concept; it is never fully achieved anywhere. According to our estimate the central item in democracy is the ballot box, where one many choose between two candidates. The Yugoslavs would argue that democracy is not only political, but economic and social. Social services such as medical aid, opportunity for education, cradle-to-the-grave insurances, are as important as the ballot box. The trend toward economic equality is also, they would say, a decisive factor in democracy.

In the social and political sense it must be considered that most Communist countries today are moving toward "democracy." Hungary, despite the brutal suppression of its revolution in 1956 by the Soviet tanks, has made impressive progress in this direction, in many respects like that of Yugoslavia. So has Poland, and, to a lesser extent, Rumania and the other Eastern European Communist nations. All, it seems evident, are adopting features of Titoism, including the Soviet Union itself, for the Liberman economic theses are, in fact, Russian adaptations of some of the Yugoslav principles.

Anyway, the changes in the Communist world must be rescued from ideological debate and put into focus in terms of human beings. I have a friend in Yugoslavia named Mila Vlasevic, whom I have known for a decade and a half. Mila is a beautiful young lady, six feet tall, still looking for a husband, and totally apolitical. When she picks up *Borba* she turns first to fashion items in the back of the paper and advertisements of television sets and furniture. She cares not one whit for ideology and has persistently refused to join the League of Communists. The first time I met her in 1953 she and her mother were living in one room of a three-room apartment, sharing bathroom and kitchen with two other families. She earned 8,000 dinar a month, owned only two dresses—one for work, one for dates—one pair of shoes and one pocketbook. In the successive times I have seen her, her life has improved dramatically. The last time I visited Belgrade she and her mother occupied a three-room apartment overlooking the river, with private kitchen and bathroom. She now earned 32,000 dinar a month and owned dozens of dresses and suits. Each year she travels to Italy or Germany on vacation where she buys still more; and the last time I saw Mila, in 1964, she told me she had stopped buying underwear in Italy because she now could buy it as cheaply in Yugoslavia, and of equal quality. The first time I talked with her, in 1953, she would not commit herself as to Tito or Titoism; the last time she was a fervid Titoist, though she had absolutely no opinions on political subjects.

Freedom, too, must be judged apart from generalities —or the criteria of the Cold War. One aspect of it is negative—the reduction of repression; the other is positive—accrual of rights. In both respects, though primarily in the first one, there have been major changes in the Communist countries of Europe. On my first trip to Yugoslavia in 1950 no one would speak with a foreigner. I recall a one-legged man with whom I conversed in German outside my hotel; after two minutes he pleaded to be left alone because "they will question me about this talk." On my last trip to the country it was possible for a foreigner to visit any home, go dancing with Yugoslav friends, and argue politics with Yugoslav intellectuals. And while one could deplore the fact that Djilas was in jail it was nonetheless possible to discuss his ideas as freely as it is possible to discuss them at any American university. Similarly in Budapest and Warsaw, though there were still fears that unorthodoxy might cramp a person's career, there was no dearth of people who would speak freely on any subject. The midnight knock, the mass arrests, the purge trials, the severe state controls are things of the past in most of these countries. The Soviet Union, as Edward Crankshaw and Averill Harriman have both noted, is moving toward a species of democracy, and its so-called satellites are moving with it. There are still repressive features to nations like Albania, East Germany, and China, but, it seems to me, here too change is inevitable as the economic and political difficulties are conquered.

Much has been made of the "cultural revolution" in China. We are told of beatings, killings, purges. No one can tell how much of this is true, how much is wild exaggeration. It is urgent, however, to put the Chinese question in focus. This is a nation that suffered incredible famines throughout its history, where the GNP before 1949 was on the order of fifteen or twenty billion dollars, and hunger was rampant. More, it is a country surrounded by American air bases, suffering daily flights by U-2's over its territory, frequently invaded by commandos from Taiwan, and heavily involved in the wars around its borders—Vietnam, Korea, and Thailand. China complains of hundreds of incidents against its shipping, instigated, it says, by the American Seventh Fleet. It is a nation in the early stages of industrialization and immensely insecure.

If the Chinese brand of communism is more militant than that of the Soviets it is understandable. Like the Soviet Union in the 1920's it feels threatened, and it is anxious to develop its domestic economy to the point where it can defend itself from what it believes will almost certainly be an American invasion. Hence, internally, it is calling on its people to make sacrifices on behalf of economic development. The cultural revolution refers to "moral" incentives as against "material" incentives. We may not like the way it is changing its people's attitudes on this score, or purging those leaders who think in other terms, but we must concede that there is a quality of idealism to "moral" incentives. The whole world, in fact, capitalist, Communist, or neutralist, is grappling with this problem: Can the human animal survive, can he avoid wars and imperialism, unless he is guided by moral concern for his fellowman and the citizens of other nations? The first AFL President, Samuel Gompers, in defining labor's goals put it in a single word—"more." But the quest for more always conflicts with the desires of other people and other nations for more, and in our century has led to far too many wars and violent social upheavals. If we were not so consumed by the Cold War we might recognize that China has put its finger on the pivotal problem facing mankind, and we might consider reducing tensions vis-à-vis this great country so that it might pursue this interesting experiment to see whether man's attitudes can be remolded to the principles of brotherhood which have been the cornerstone of idealism, religious and lay, since the dawn of civilization.

In external relations the Chinese feel they are under far greater pressure than any nation in the world. They react to this therefore by stirring the revolutionary pot against "American imperialism" wherever they can; and they berate the Soviets for not sharing atomic secrets with them or contributing adequately to what they consider a common defense against the United States. Innumerable China experts have argued that China would like to concentrate on internal development, and that if left alone it would take a softer course. History has proven conclusively, it seems to me, that when Communist nations have felt more secure they have adopted less repressive measures at home. So that whatever is going on in China today—and frankly, no one in the United States really knows—it must be clear that its potential for change will be greatly influenced by whether we in the West take a more benign or a harsher attitude toward dealing with it.

In addition to the Chinese, Soviet, Yugoslav, and East European forms of communism (leaving aside the emerging forms in the non-Communist world), there is finally the Cuban form. It differs from the Soviet and Yugoslav types in that it stresses "moral" incentives; it frankly asks its people to make sacrifices on behalf of the future. It seems to differ from the Chinese brand in that it has not resorted to repression in the same way or on the same scale. It is a uniquely Latin-American and nationalist communism that has far more appeal for the leftist youth of the world than any other communism today, and may very well emerge, once the blockade and other measures against it are relaxed, as the leader of a third world force—neither pro-Moscow nor pro-Peking on the one hand, and certainly not pro-Washington on the other.

What do all these changes in the Communist world and the emergence of polycentrism mean?

165

First, it seems clear that communism is a much more stable system than it has been at any time in the last half-century. It has far stronger economies, it provides far better for its people than we have been led to believe, and it has greater self-confidence. It is changing precisely because life is becoming easier in most Communist nations, not harder, and those who still think it will erupt from within and be overthrown are badly misguided.

Our image of the Communist nations is unfortunately as warped as their image of us has been. I recall arguing in 1950 with a Yugoslav labor leader who claimed that "thousands" of Negroes were lynched in the United States each year, and when I told him that even though the Negro is terribly abused this was a wild exaggeration, I'm sure he considered me an agent of Wall Street. On the other hand, in 1960 when I returned from the Soviet Union, I had a conversation with a waiter in a restaurant on Lexington Avenue in New York who had equally wild pictures of life in Moscow. The waiter wanted to know where we had come from, and when we said the Soviet Union he expressed disbelief. Whereupon I showed him a ruble that I had taken out with me. The man seemed stunned. "Do they use money in Russia?" "Of course," I said. "What do you think they use?" He replied, "I've always been under the impression that Russians work twelve or fourteen hours a day, and are then locked up at night, given food and clothes, but not permitted out. They don't need money. You know, it's a slave society." Naïve as was this estimate, and even allowing that it is not shared by many, it nonetheless indicates how we accept almost subliminally our own pernicious propaganda about how "the other side" lives.

This image does not square with fact. The Communist lands not only use money, but their GNP's are growing sensationally and they are becoming, more rapidly than any other segment of the developing areas, "have" nations.

Secondly, the Communist world is here to stay. It will be modified, altered, remolded toward greater economic and political democracy, but it won't be overthrown either from within or from without. The Communist regimes are not as unpopular with their people as our public information officers pretend. It is worth noting that while every single adult in North Vietnam has a gun in his hand Ho Chi-minh can walk amongst them with less fear of assassination than President Johnson or the late President Kennedy. Or, that while a half million Cubans are armed with weapons—the largest militia in the Western Hemisphere—no effort has been made by them to topple the Castro government, and so far as I know there has been no killing of an important Cuban leader, though they circulate often amongst the male and female militia.

Communism is here to stay, just as capitalism was here to stay after its revolutions in the seventeenth, eighteenth, and nineteenth centuries. The Austrian Prince Metternich, at the beginning of the nineteenth century, believed that the capitalist revolution could be rolled back. He forged a "Holy Alliance" of the reactionary feudal states of Europe to prevent national revolutions in Poland, Latin America, Spain, Austria, and elsewhere, and for a time enjoyed some success. The Polish revolution was smashed; the wave of rebellions in 1830 resulted in defeat for European nationalists. But the French and American revolutions could not be reversed, though Metternich dreamed of it; and even wars of national liberation in Latin America could not be abrogated. By 1848 the revolutionary tidal wave swept Prince Metternich himself into the dustbin of history.

We live today in an era of revolution—five dozen nationalist uprisings and peaceful revolutions (such as those in India or Burma) since the end of the war. Communism is part of that national revolutionary cycle. Its strength lies in attaching itself to this historical wave, not in its abstract doctrine of historical materialism or surplus value. Not a single one of the postwar revolutions has been a "proletarian revolution," not even the one in China. All have been nationalist revolts, and where communism has won additional victories (China, Yugoslavia, Cuba, Vietnam, and elsewhere) it has been because it attached itself to the nationalist apirations. Since this nationalism is certain to succeed, it is futile to think that the Communist force that has joined it can be extirpated by military means.

America's reliance on military force as the "answer" to communism has in fact been communism's best ally. For it has forced Washington to form alliances—for bases and support—with innumerable reactionary regimes. Those reactionary regimes cannot survive in a world that is in revolution, and as one after another falls the American position becomes more tenuous, and the Communist position stronger. There are two to two and a half billion people in our world living on fifty to two-hundred dollars a year. They can no longer be side-tracked by empty clichés about democracy, useless anti-communist rhetoric, or military occupation.

Further, the Communist nations cannot be occupied by military force, as events in Vietnam indicate. The United States and its allies, with one and two-tenths million troops, are unable to subdue the National Libera-tion Front and its North Vietnamese ally, with forces only one-fourth as large, without planes, without any-where near the American firepower. And if this is true in Indochina, it is far more true of China. How can China be conquered? One small group of rightist Ameri-cans believes it can be done by dropping nuclear bombs on it, in a preventive war. But that obviously would lead to innumerable deaths from fallout in Japan, Siberia, and, very likely, Europe and the United States; and it not only could not kill off all of China's seven hundred and fifty million people but would lead to world nuclear war. In such a war, President Kennedy has told us, there would be ninety million dead Americans within eighteen hours, no matter who pushed the first button. Nor can China be conquered by a land force. China is a million villages. In any external attack it could easily mobilize two guerrillas from each village (in Vietnam, the Viet Cong recruit about fifteen). According to Col. George M. Jones, a leading American expert on guerrilla war, it takes ten to fifteen troops to contain one guerrilla. The United States would need not a half million men as in Vietnam or thirty billion dollars a year, but twenty to thirty million troops, and expenditures in the hundreds of billions. It is a completely impossible situation, not the least because it would bankrupt the United States and end all semblance of democracy. And far from overthrowing Mao and his fellow-Chinese leaders, it would doubtless, as in North Vietnam, consolidate the people behind him.

Finally, it is useless to think that the schisms within communism—its polycentrism—can result in its demise. There may or may not be war between the Soviet Union and China eventually—though much of American observation on this score is wishful thinking—but in any case communism will remain an attractive force for the nations in the third world, and very likely increasingly so. Each type of communism is today developing its own allies in this third world—Tito with Egypt and India, China with certain African states, Cuba with Latin American revolutionaries, and the Soviet Union with a host of nations and forces. To think that communism is unpopular because it is not democratic in our sense is another form of beguiling wishful thinking. Almost all the developing nations have never known democracy. What they see in communism is a force that has succeeded in nations similar to theirs, and it is for this that they frequently look up to it. Communism is answering the same questions they are called on to answer.

The changing character of communism imposes on us the necessity of reevaluating our strategy. That reevaluation should have been done long ago, but it becomes more urgent with every passing day, and more obvious with every modification of the Communist systems. The sooner we arrive at an overall thesis that we have no alternative but to find means of coexisting with this phenomenon, the more secure we can build the American fortress, now breached at many points. To continue along the present lines, to fail to grasp the significance of changes in the Communist world, may lead to our own eclipse, through nuclear war or otherwise.

The Contributors

Thomas W. Ogletree is Associate Professor of Constructive Theology at Chicago Theological Seminary. His other books include *Christian Faith and History: A Critical Comparison of Ernst Troeltsch and Karl Barth* and *The Death of God Controversy.*

Jürgen Moltmann, Professor of Systematic Theology at the University of Tübingen, has authored numerous books. Two have been translated into English: *The Theology of Hope* and *Two Studies in the Theology of Bonhoeffer* (which he co-authored).

Charles C. West is Professor of Christian Ethics at Princeton Theological Seminary. Other books by him are *Communism and the Theologians* and *Outside the Camp*.

Paul Lehmann is Auburn Professor of Systematic Theology at Union Theological Seminary. He is the author of *Forgiveness, Decisive Issue in Protestant Thought; Re-educating Germany; Ethics in a Christian Context*.

Sidney Lens is a free-lance writer and former union official. His many books include *the Crisis of American Labor; Africa, Awakening Giant; The Futile Crusade; Radicalism in America; A Country Is Born*.